THE TRAIL OF THE DINOSAUR

& Other Essays

This new collection of essays by Arthur Koestler is a continuation, chronologically and by subject matter, of his earlier brilliant collection called *The Yogi and the Commissar,* published a decade ago.

"At that time," writes Koestler, "when victory, at long last, had just come in sight, the Western world was full of illusions . . . " Probably no one has more forcefully or concisely defined those illusions than Koestler himself, so much of whose writing has been devoted to the most urgent question of our postwar world: the survival of free man.

The selections in this volume, with one exception, date from 1946 to 1955. Some of their titles are: The Challenge of Our Time; The Candles of Truth; The Seven Deadly Fallacies; and The Little Flirts—a devastating exposé of pseudo-intellectual leftist dilettantes. Other pieces range in subject from Whittaker Chambers to George Orwell, from a dissertation on snobbery to a consideration of Science Fiction and a speculation on the future of the novel. The penultimate essay, entitled A Guide to Political Neuroses, in which he equates politics with the psychopathology of sex, is Koestler at his satirical and incisive best; and the final essay, from which the book derives its title, is a deeply moving and utterly serious summation of man's predicament in today's explosive world.

THE TRAIL
OF THE DINOSAUR

& Other Essays

BY

ARTHUR KOESTLER

NEW YORK

THE MACMILLAN COMPANY

1955

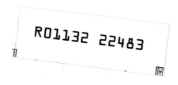

First Printing

Printed in the United States of America

CONTENTS

Contents

PREFACE

1

THE ESSAYS, lectures and broadcast talks in this book date from 1946 to 1955 and are a sequel to a previous collection, *The Yogi and the Commissar*, completed in 1944. At that time the Western world lived in the euphoria of approaching victory, and the pessimistic forecasts in that volume were almost unanimously rejected as fantasies of a morbid imagination. In the ten years that have passed since *The Yogi and the Commissar* was published, all its pessimistic and seemingly absurd predictions have come true, but none of its optimistic and seemingly plausible ones—few and cautious though the latter were.

2

"The typical career of the French politician", I wrote some years ago, "reads like a book, from left to right." Though I am not a French politician, the evolution reflected in these essays could be regarded as a confirmation of that rule—if the words "left" and "right" still possessed any concrete political meaning. One of the submissions of the present volume is that they have lost that meaning, and that man, if he is to survive, must shift the focus of his eyes to more vital questions.

Preface

This book, then, is a farewell to arms. The last essays and speeches in it that deal directly with political questions date from 1950, and are now five years old. Since then I felt that I have said all I had to say on these questions which had obsessed me, in various ways, for the best part of a quarter-century. Now the errors are atoned for, the bitter passion has burnt itself out; Cassandra has gone hoarse, and is due for a vocational change.

London, February 1955.

I

THE CHALLENGE

"The Challenge of our Time"

Opening talk of a BBC broadcast series, Spring, 1947

I WOULD like to start with a story—it is a story which you all know, but it will lead us straight to the heart of our problem.

On the 18th of January, 1912, Captain Scott and his four companions reached the South Pole, after a march of sixty-nine days. On the return journey Petty Officer Evans fell ill, and became a burden to the party. Captain Scott had to make a decision. Either he carried the sick man along, slowed down the march and risked perdition for all; or he let Evans die alone in the wilderness and tried to save the rest. Scott took the first course; they dragged Evans along until he died. The delay proved fatal. The blizzards overtook them; Oates, too, fell ill and sacrificed himself; their rations were exhausted; and the frozen bodies of the four men were found six months later only ten miles, or one day's march, from the next depot which they had been unable to reach. Had they sacrificed Evans, they would probably have been saved.

This dilemma, which faced Scott under eighty degrees of latitude, symbolises the eternal predicament of man, the tragic conflict inherent in his nature. It is the conflict between expediency and morality. I shall try to show that this conflict is at the root of our political and social crisis, that it contains in a nutshell the challenge of our time.

Scott had the choice between two roads. Let us follow each of

11

them into their logical extensions. First, the road of expediency, where the traveller is guided by the principle that the End justifies the Means. He starts with throwing Evans to the wolves, as the sacrifice of one comrade is justified by the hope of saving four. As the road extends into the field of politics, the dilemma of Captain Scott becomes the dilemma of Mr. Chamberlain. Evans is Czechoslovakia; the sacrifice of this small nation will buy the safety of bigger ones—or so it is hoped. We continue on the straight, logical metal road which now leads us from Munich No. 1 to Munich No. 2: the Ribbentrop-Molotov Pact of 1939, where the Poles go the way the Czechs have gone. By that time the number of individual Evanses is counted by the million: in the name of expediency the German Government decides to kill all incurables and mentally deficients. They are a drag on the nation's sledge and rations are running short. After the incurables come those with bad heredity—Gypsies and Jews: six millions of them. Finally, in the name of expediency, the Western democracies let loose the first atomic bombs on the crowded towns of Hiroshima and Nagasaki, and thus implicitly accept the principle of total and indiscriminate warfare which they hitherto condemned. We continue on our logical road, which has now become a steep slope, into the field of party politics. If you are convinced that a political opponent will lead your country into ruin and plunge the world into a new war—is it not preferable that you should forget your scruples and try to discredit him by revelations about his private life, frame him, blacken him, purge him, censor him, deport, him, liquidate him? Unfortunately, your opponent will be equally convinced that you are harmful, and use the same methods against you. Thus, the logic of expediency leads to the atomic disintegration of morality, a kind of radioactive decay of all values.

And now let us turn to the second alternative before Scott. This road leads into the opposite direction; its guiding principles are: respect for the individual, the rejection of violence, and the belief that the Means determine the End. We have seen what happened to Scott's expedition because he did *not* sacrifice Evans. And we can imagine what would have happened to the people of India had Mr. Gandhi been allowed to have his saintly way of non-resistance to the Japanese invader; or what would have been the fate of this country had it embraced pacifism, and with it the Gestapo with headquarters in Whitehall.

The fact that both roads lead to disaster, creates a dilemma which is inseparable from man's condition; it is not an invention of the philosophers, but a conflict which we face at each step in our daily affairs. Each of us has sacrificed his Evans at one point or another of his past. And it is a fallacy to think that the conflict can always be healed by that admirable British household ointment called "the reasonable compromise". Compromise is a useful thing in minor dilemmas of daily routine; but each time we face major decisions, the remedy lets us down. Neither Captain Scott nor Mr. Chamberlain could fall back on a reasonable compromise. The more responsible the position you hold, the sharper you feel the horns of the dilemma. When a decision involves the fate of a great number of people, the conflict grows proportionately. The technical progress of our age has enormously increased the range and consequence of man's actions, and has thus amplified his inherent dilemma to gigantic proportions. This is the reason for our awareness of a crisis. We resemble the patient who hears for the first time, magnified by a loudspeaker, the erratic thundering of his heart.

The dilemma admits no final solution. But each period has to attempt a temporary solution adapted to its own condition. That attempt has to proceed in two steps. The first is to realise that a certain admixture of ruthlessness is inseparable from human progress. Without the rebellion of the Barons, there would be no Magna Carta; without the storming of the Bastille, no proclamation of the Rights of Man. The more we have moral values at heart, the more we should beware of crankiness. The trouble with some well-meaning ethical movements is that they have so many sectarians and quietists and cranks in their midst.

But the second and more important step is to realise that the End only justifies the Means within very narrow limits. A surgeon is justified in inflicting pain because the results of the operation are reasonably predictable; but drastic large-scale operations on the social body involve many unknown factors, lead to unpredictable results, and one never knows at what point the surgeon's lancet turns into the butcher's hatchet. Or, to change the metaphor: ruthlessness is like arsenic; injected in very small doses it is a stimulant to the social body, in large quantities it is deadly poison. And to-day we are all suffering from moral arsenic poisoning.

The symptoms of this disease are obvious in the political and social field; they are less obvious but no less dangerous in the field of science and philosophy. Let me quote as an example the opinions of one of our leading physicists, Professor J. D. Bernal. In an article called "Belief and Action" recently published by the *Modern Quarterly*, he says that "the new social relations" require "a radical change in morality", and that the virtues "based on excessive concern with individual rectitude" need readjustment by a "change from individual to collective morality". "Because collective action is the only effective action, it is the only virtuous action", says Professor Bernal. Now let us see what this rather abstract statement really means. The only practical way for Tom, Dick or Harry to take "effective collective action" is to become a member of an army, political party or movement. His choice will be determined (a) by his nationality, and (b) by his political opinions or prejudices. Once he has joined the collective of his choice, he has to subordinate his "individual rectitude" to the interests of the group or party. This is precisely what, for instance, the accused in the Belsen Trial did. Their excuse was that they had to service the gas chamber and push the victims into it out of loyalty to their party, because their individual responsibility was subordinated to collective responsibility. Counsel for the Defence of Irma Grese could have quoted verbatim Professor Bernal's reflections on ethics—though politically Bernal is a staunch opponent of Nazism and supports, to quote his own words, "the theories of Marx and the practice of Lenin and Stalin". His article actually contains some reservations to the effect that there should be no question of "blind and obedient carrying out of orders", which, he says, leads to the *Führerprinzip*. He does not seem to have noticed that blind obedience plus the *Führerprinzip* are nowhere more in evidence to-day than in the Party to which Professor Bernal's sympathies belong. In short, I believe that much confusion could be avoided if some scientists would stick to their electrons and realise that human beings do not fit into mathematical equations. And it should be realised that this is not an abstract philosophical quarrel, but a burning and very concrete issue on which it depends whether our civilisation shall live or die.

Let me return to my starting-point, the dilemma between expediency and morality. In the course of our discussion, the symbolic sledge of Scott's small party has grown into the express train of mankind's progress. On this train expediency is the engine, morality the brake. The action of the two is always antagonistic. We cannot make an abstract decision in favour of one or the other. But we can make temporary adjustments according to the train's progress. Two hundred years ago, during the train's laborious ascent from the stagnant marshes of feudal France towards the era of the Rights of Man, the decision would have been in favour of the engine and against the brake. Since about the second half of the nineteenth century our ethical brakes have been more and more neglected until totalitarian dynamism made the engine run amok. We must apply the brake or we shall crash.

The Challenge

I am not sure whether what the philosophers call ethical absolutes exist, but I am sure that we have to act as if they existed. Ethics must be freed from its utilitarian chains; words and deeds must again be judged on their own merits and not as mere make-shifts to serve distant and nebulous aims. These worm-eaten ladders lead to no paradise.

A Way to Fight Suspicion*

1

IN 1938 we were appeasing the German mania of grandeur; to-day we are appeasing the Russian mania of persecution. Yet as long as this pathological condition lasts, all hope for genuine world co-operation is illusory.

During the war, pressure was brought upon our Press and Radio not to utter any criticism which might upset our Soviet ally's delicate temper. Books critical of the Stalin régime were withdrawn from publishers' lists; any mention of the fact that it was a dictatorship, any reference to Russia being communistic, or having ceased to be communistic, wanting international revolution, or abandoning international revolution, had to be carefully avoided. The Press, led by Lord Beaverbrook, built up the myth of jovial "Uncle Joe" whose pipe outrivalled in popularity even Churchill's cigar and Roosevelt's cigarette holder.

But as it passed through the filter of the Soviet censorship and through the controlled channels of the Tass Agency, the gentle cooing of the Western voices became transformed into the barking of mad imperialist dogs. The Battle of Britain and of the Seas, the campaigns in North Africa and Italy, were played down by the filter until they were hardly audible, while the clamour for the "second" front gave the Russian people the impression that there was only one, and that they were fighting the war alone.

---

* First published in *The New York Times*, 10 March, 1946.

The majority of Soviet citizens have never heard of Dunkirk, of Bataan, of Alamein; what they heard were reports from Cairo that the British were negotiating a separate peace, that the Americans were dropping arms to the Fascist Warsaw *maquis*, and that we were sitting back in our armchairs watching the Russian people bleed to death. Nothing that the Western powers did or did not do, nothing that they said or did not say, could influence Russian suspicions—for they are an artificial growth, a hot-house plant unaffected by the real temperature outside the glass walls.

What historical reasons prompted the leaders of the Soviet State to create systematically, from 1918 onwards, this artificial climate? They did it certainly neither out of stupidity nor of malevolence. Hitler and Goebbels whipped the Germans into mass-hysteria because they were preparing for war. But the paramount factor in Soviet policy up to 1941 was to keep out of war at any price, even at the price of the Hitler-Stalin pact of 1939.

There were two reasons why the common man in the U.S.S.R. had to be vaccinated with the serum of distrust against foreign influences. The first was external, the second internal.

The external reason was, in the early days, real enough to warrant caution in dealings with the capitalistic world. The Western powers had supported the armies of the counter-revolution during the Civil War of 1917-21; they persecuted Communists; they waited hopefully for the collapse of the Soviet régime and tried in various ways to speed it up; the reactionary press spread shameless lies about conditions in Russia and depicted the young, suffering, struggling country as a giant brothel run by drunks and nun-raping sadists. All this gave the infant revolution a kind of traumatic shock. To live it down would in any case have taken considerable time. For internal reasons, which I shall discuss presently, the Soviet leaders were interested not in living down, but in perpetuating the trauma. They kept the memory of the "Capitalist Intervention", the slogans of an "Anti-Soviet

18

Crusade", and of the *"Cordon Sanitaire"* ever-present in the people's mind; they systematically developed it into an obsession.

Now let us compare this development with the evolution of public opinion in the West. The Western countries had, of course, as sound reasons to be suspicious of Russia as the other way round. Up to the middle 'thirties the avowed aim of the Communist International was the violent overthrow of their régimes. The wave of strikes and abortive revolutions which swept over the world in the wake of the Russian revolution provided the equivalent traumatic shock for the countries of the West.

However, by the middle 'thirties the average common man with average common sense had lived down that trauma. He was able to do that because a free press, free discussion, uncensored books, had gradually enabled him to see things in their proper perspective, enabled him to see that Russia really wanted peace to build up her industry, that her support of world revolution had become half- or rather quarter-hearted, and that the Communists outside Russia were a vocal, idealistic and rather pathetic band, who were martyred in Germany and Eastern Europe without Moscow lifting a finger to help them, while in the West they were more a nuisance than a danger. The persecution-maniacs in the West who still lived on the Red Scare had by that time become a dwindling, reactionary minority. The majority were convinced that despite the difference in social and political structure, the Soviets and the West could do business with each other and find a stable *modus vivendi*.

Thus the original shock was gradually lived down in the West, while it was artificially fanned and preserved by the centralised propaganda apparatus of the Soviets. Why? We now come to the internal causes for this attitude.

19

2

The transformation of Soviet Eurasia from a backward agrarian to a modern industrial country was a gigantic task which required gigantic sacrifices imposed upon the population. These included exporting food and raw materials to pay for imported machinery, and concentrating on heavy industry instead of producing commodities. The five-year plans, instead of lifting, had to lower the living standard of the people. To the leaders this was a logical and unavoidable consequence of their long-term policy. But it would have been too much to expect the illiterate masses to understand the paradox that the workers and peasants in a socialist country were worse off in food, clothing and housing than the workers and peasants under the capitalist yoke. The opportunity of making comparisons would have meant a constant provocation and would have overtaxed the ordinary man's powers of thinking in abstractions. Russia had embarked on an unprecedented adventure, leaving the fleshpots of Egypt behind, and it was only logical that the fleshpots should be kept out of the people's sight while they were led through the desert towards the distant goal. Thus the iron curtain was lowered round Russia. No Soviet citizen, except on special mission, was allowed to leave the frontiers of his country, or to make friends with foreign journalists and engineers in Russia. Non-fraternisation was the motto of Russian contacts with the outside world during the lifetime of a whole generation. The State monopoly in information, the campaigns and stunt-trials against "foreign saboteurs", gave the Russian people a grotesquely distorted picture of conditions in the West. In this hot-house climate of propaganda, the seeds of suspicion sprouted into a tropical plant.

3

So much for the genesis of suspicion. What can we do to break it down?

Mere gestures of goodwill are futile. If to-morrow the complete blueprints of our atom plants were handed unconditionally on a silver plate to M. Vishinsky, *Pravda* would inform the Russian people that "the irresistible pressure of the Communist Party and of the toiling masses had forced the imperialist American Government to capitulate to their demands"; and things would go on exactly as before.

Some people set their hopes on the returning Russian soldiers who, by spreading the news of what they saw abroad, would gradually wear down the barrier. I think one should not over-estimate this hope. Once demobilised and dispersed, the veterans will again be submitted to the climate of the propaganda hot-house, and after a year or so they will forget their experiences, as they had forgotten by 1941 that in 1939 Moscow radio called England and France the aggressors in the imperialist war against Germany.

In short, palliatives will not help. The Soviet Government has achieved, for the first time in history, a complete State monopoly not only over the production and distribution of goods, but also over the production and distribution of ideas, opinions and emotions. World peace can only become a reality if suspicion is abolished. Suspicion can only be abolished if the Soviet Government can be induced to turn the master-switch of their propaganda factory.

How can the Soviet leaders be induced to do this? The first necessity is that our own statesmen should realise that no political treaties and trade agreements can guarantee peace as long as this world remains psychologically divided into two worlds, with persecution-mania on one side, growing alarm on the other. The conclusion and aim of this article is a plea to politicians for the inclusion of the psychological factor in their power-calculations, as a factor equal in importance to Air Forces and Navies. More precisely: *that psychological armaments should be made an object of international negotiations and of political bargaining just as armaments in the air and on the sea; and made subject to as clearly defined clauses as, for instance, naval armaments are.*

By "psychological armaments" I do *not* mean criticism directed by one country against another. This democratic right is as vital on the international as on the national scale, and such criticism cannot do much harm if the country criticised has full facilities of stating its case before the public of the country from which the criticism comes. But it becomes poisonous if the country attacked is deprived of this right of defence—as the Western countries are at present in the Soviet Press, which prints M. Vishinsky's speeches but suppresses Bevin's replies, prints statements by E.L.A.S. but suppresses those by the Greek Government, and so on.

The measure of "psychological armament" is the extent to which a government obstructs the free exchange of information and ideas with the outside world. A country which builds a Maginot line of censorship from behind which it fires its propaganda salvoes is committing psychological aggression.

Since the end of the war, the U.S.S.R. has raised certain claims in South-Eastern Europe, the Middle and Far East and North Africa. The Western Powers, who have no territorial counter-claims to make, should table instead a demand for *psychological disarmament*, including:

    (a) free access of foreign newspapers, periodicals, books and films to the U.S.S.R.;

    (b) such modifications of the Russian censorship (if censorship there must be) as to permit the free circulation of information about the outside world throughout Soviet territory;

(c) free access for accredited journalists, parliamentary committees, etc., to Russian-occupied territory;

(d) the abolishing of restrictions on travel for foreigners in Soviet territory, and for Soviet citizens abroad;

(e) active co-operation with the Western Powers in the organisation of "vacations abroad" schemes, on a mutual exchange basis, for students, teachers, writers, workers and professional men.

4

I do not know whether this is a counter-revolutionary, Trotskyite or Fascist suggestion; but I do know that if it were carried out, if the doors of the hot-house were opened to the sun and fresh air of the world's natural climate, the next war (which will mean the end of us all, including the people of Russia) could be avoided.

The European Continent, emerging from four years of Nazi occupation, is a shambles; its standard of living has fallen below the level of Tsarist Russia—thus, the Soviet leaders have no longer any reason, as in the pre-war decades, to fear misleading comparisons if the iron curtain is lifted. Psychological disarmament would almost automatically lead to material disarmament, and the enormous Soviet potential thus diverted into productive channels would lead to a rapid rise of the standard of living of the Russian people, and make isolation the more superfluous. The present vicious circle would be reversed. If I were a politician, I would gladly swap the North Persian oil, plus a trusteeship in North Africa, for the acceptance of these demands.

Nobody in his senses will expect the Soviet leaders to agree to this easily. Hence the suggestion that psychological disarmament should be made a bargaining object in all future negotiations, and given high priority on the political agenda. The demand for the free circulation of ideas across frontiers, for restoring the arrested bloodstream of the world, should be raised at every meeting of the Big Three, the Security Council, the Committees and Assembly of the United Nations; it should be made the pre-condition of concessions in the geographical, economical and scientific field. To get it accepted, the use of all levers of pressure, political and economical, would for once be morally justified.

Land of Virtue and Gloom*

London, November, 1946
DEAR EDITORS,

If governments are to be remembered by epithets like "the Hundred Days", or "the Terror", this first government of the socialist era in Britain will pass into history as the Reign of Virtuous Gloom. Both, the virtue and the gloom, become strikingly evident if one compares our life here with conditions in France (whence I have just returned after a long visit). The contrast is truly remarkable.

France has emerged from five years of occupation in a state of almost complete economic sanity and moral insanity. She produces most of the food she needs, but the normal channels of circulation and distribution have broken down. This breakdown is due not to economic, but to political and moral causes. In other words, it is a functional, not a structural disease. There is plenty of wheat but little bread, because the farmers feed wheat to the cattle, distrusting the franc; there is plenty of milk, but not a drop in Paris, for similar reasons; there are plenty of consumer-goods, but prices soar because the goods are speculatively hoarded. During my six weeks' stay, there were six *scandales* or exposures of large-scale rackets in bread, wine, potatoes, pulse, petrol, and clothing coupons—each *scandale* implicating one of

* Condensed version of three "London Letters", published by *Partisan Review*, New York, in 1947-48.

25

the political parties in the then tripartite government and being launched by one of the rival parties at the appropriate moment, as a routine move on the political chess-board. There is no longer a black market as it has practically swallowed the legal white one; the result is a general grey of various shades, expressing the degrees of illegality of the transactions to which the ordinary Frenchman is driven in order to obtain bread, fats, meat, apartments, clothes, cigarettes; and to obtain the money for obtaining them. The same routine of lawbreaking is forced upon shopkeepers, department stores, and business firms if they want to survive. Even the political parties were cashing in on the black market according to the production-branch they controlled through their ministries; the most notorious case was the sale of licences for the acquisition of private cars by the Communist Minister of Production, Marcel Paul, in return for contributions to the Party fund. Rationing had broken down so completely that nobody whom I asked even knew what the official rations were on which he was supposed to live. This inevitably led to the retort whether I knew what *our* rations were and whether *we* lived on them; and affirmative answers met with frank incredulity or a polite smile, implying that I was trying to sell British propaganda. But there was also a curious resentment, betraying some half-conscious national guilt complex, and expressed by sneers at the priggish virtues and lack of *débrouillardise* of the British. But, of course, not all Frenchmen have the knack of *débrouillardise* —so much the worse for them. As a public figure said: Two-thirds of France live in the jungle, the remaining third in the desert.

I repeat—and the fact is publicly admitted by the more sincere French politicians—that all this is due not to economic, but to political and moral causes. Medicine had to recognise that there are functional disorders without demonstrable structural defects; social science will probably arrive at similar conclusions.

Land of Virtue and Gloom

Meanwhile I submit the matter for discussion in your symposium on "the future of socialism".

To return to this island of Virtue and Gloom: if you reverse the present condition of France, then you get roughly the idea of the present condition of England. From the economic point of view, England emerged from the war very nearly bankrupt. But at the first post-war elections it recorded the sanest vote in its history; and public morale, in accepting continued rationing and austerity, proved almost depressingly sound and firm. I say depressingly, because this patient acceptance is not so much based on foresight and voluntary sacrifice, as on resignation, puritan tradition, and lack of *joie de vivre*. The people in the suburbs and working-class districts accept the bad life because they have never tasted the good life; there is probably more rejoicing in heaven about one repentant French black marketeer than about ten British Ministry of Food Inspectors.

Still, one can't have it both ways, and the English chose the hard and sound one. In France, the contrast between rich and poor has become sharply accentuated since the war; here nobody starves and nobody gets a decent steak. This is meant literally: even in London's top luxury restaurants food is much poorer, both in quality and quantity, than in the average French *bistro*. The black market here is insignificant; though scarce goods are kept under the counter for old customers, they are sold at regulation price, and it is quite impossible, for instance, to buy a packet of cigarettes by offering more money for it—whereas in France any amount can be had by paying four times the official price.

In short, the socialist era in Britain started by a general levelling down of the living standard—precisely as the stupidest critics of socialist theory had predicted. Needless to say, this is not the Government's fault, but the aftermath of war and of decades of capitalist mismanagement (of the coal mines, for instance). Needless to say, too, this is cold comfort in an English winter marked by coal cuts, gas cuts, ration cuts, cigarette shortage, beer shortage, and by the dull, monotonous "more austerity" warnings of the leaders, who seem to have retained nothing from the brilliant flow of Churchillian rhetoric except the sweat-and-toil motif. The irony of the situation is, that while the higher income classes (down to the skilled worker and small shopkeeper) suffer acutely from the levelling-down process, the lower income classes are not conscious of "going up". For their benefits are relative, not absolute: rationing does not give them more food, but merely prevents their getting even less; government-controlled building re-houses only a fraction of the bombed-out per year and merely prevents all building material from going to the rich; and so on. The objective impoverishment of the country makes it inevitable that the hardships caused by socialist policy are real, the benefits mainly theoretical. The consequence of all this is growing apathy and resignation. As a symbol of contemporary Britain the lion and the unicorn could be replaced by the varicose veins of the British housewife after six years of queueing. But as neither Tories nor Communists have any attractive alternative to offer, the keynote of the people's mood is resentment, not revolt; except for a few, so far isolated episodes—squatting, small mutinies against demobilisation delays overseas, and a series of unauthorised strikes—about which more below.

After eighteen months of Labour rule it is, of course, too early to draw conclusions. But it is not too early to point out two basic factors among the confusing multitude of threads. One is an objective, one a subjective factor, and both are relevant to socialist theory.

The first consideration is that socialist movements are apparently doomed always to ascend to power under the worst possible objective conditions. This, on the one hand, provides socialists with the ready excuse that the theory should not be judged by experiments carried out under such handicaps. The Paris

Commune was handicapped by war, siege, and famine; the Soviet system was tried out first in the most backward country of Europe; the Weimar Republic carried the economic and psychological burden of Versailles, which broke its back. British Labour inherited the hostility of all coloured people, the bad international reputation of past colonial policies, and above all, a country economically on the verge of ruin; thus, once again, the experiment cannot provide conclusive evidence for or against the theory. It would only become conclusive, the theorist argues, if socialism could be tried out in a rich, modern industrial country, secure from external aggression—the U.S.A., for instance.

It seems to me that this argument puts the cart before the horse. You cannot expect any ruling class to hand in its resignation, nor the masses to listen to radical propaganda, while all goes well. Hence it is in the nature of things that socialist movements will always inherit a more or less bankrupt estate, that they will always ascend to power in the "wrong" country or at the "wrong" moment. As this factor is implicit in socialist theory it cannot at the same time be treated as an extraneous accident and serve as an excuse. Socialism is meant to be a cure for diseased society, and no doctor can get away with the excuse that people only call him when they are ill.

This brings us to the second factor: every leadership has a certain elbow-room of subjective freedom within the hard limits set by objective conditions. Nobody can blame the Government for being unable to provide more houses, food, coal, dollars for imports, and so on. You cannot expect socialism to do miracles—but you can and must expect it to give the people a message and an inspiration, to bring home to them the consciousness of the opening of a new era. This is where the Labour Government has completely failed. Take, as an example, the momentous event of Britain's coal mines passing from private to national ownership after half a century of socialist agitation, on

The Challenge

1st January, 1947. Coal is the hard core of Britain's industrial life, and the coal miner is the pioneer and symbol of the struggles of the working-class movement. What a pageant Hitler or Mussolini would have staged to impress upon the people's memory this historic event! What a glorious ballyhoo, if it had happened in America! Well, I have seen the great event on the newsreels. It took place in the Ministry of Fuel's austere conference room, and was about as inspiring as the annual visit of the welfare committee in a state orphanage. Shinwell's speech and Lord Hyndley's reply were in the greyest virtue-and-gloom key; and the only moment when proceedings rose to the pathos of the historic occasion came when Attlee referred to the future of the National Coal Board with the inspired metaphor: "It is going to bat on a sticky wicket, but I think it will score a great many sixes." You can imagine how elated the miners must have felt at this flash of Dantonesque oratory.

It is nonsense to pretend that people in this country don't like noisy celebrations and public displays; each Derby Day and Cup Final is proof to the contrary. It is equally stupid to keep repeating that "this is no time for celebrations". No people can live on bread-rationing alone. I am not arguing in favour of circus games; I only want to say that socialism minus emotional appeal, structural changes in economy without functional changes in mass-consciousness, must always lead to a dead end of one sort or another. The present Labour leaders do not seem to have even an inkling of this truth. While the Government passes its nationalisation bills, raises the school-leaving age, institutes its Public Health Services, votes old-age pensions and family allowances, pursues its legislative programme slowly, steadily, and on the whole with considerable success, it is doing nothing to change the atmosphere, the mental climate of the country. If a new Rip Van Winkle had gone to sleep under the Churchill Government two years ago and woke up now, he could spend weeks travelling all over England without discovering that anything has changed in people's lives. I happen to live on a sheep farm in North Wales, next to a slate-mining village called Blaenau Ffestiniog. As neither slate-mining nor sheep-farming are on the nationalisation programme, the "landslide", the "new era" has changed literally nothing in the life of the village, in the thoughts and habits and emotions of the people. The advent of the Age of Socialism has affected their daily routine about as much as a change of government in Mexico. And the same goes for millions of the politically indifferent, all over the country.

"But what else did you expect?" the staunch Labour politician will answer: "you know that we are a reformist, gradualist movement; you can't expect Clem Attlee to dance the Carmagnole in Trafalgar Square, nor Lord Rothschild, a Labour peer, to swing aristocrats on lamp-posts. You are a romantic, my dear fellow, and your idea of socialism is half a century behind the times. 'Business as usual' was our motto during the Blitz, and 'business as usual' is the motto of our Socialist Revolution. For a revolution it is, though a slow and bloodless one; and even our ultra-radical Harold Laski brought a libel suit against a newspaper which had alleged that by preaching revolution he meant anything rash or violent."

This is the typical kind of answer of the typical Labour politician, based on the typical mistake of equating gradualism with dullness. With one half of the argument I fully agree: to wit, that the reformist way is the only possible one for this country; that a revolution on orthodox Marxist lines, apart from being unthinkable under present conditions, would lead to a catastrophe; and that, if all goes well and Labour remains in power, we shall see, within a generation or so, a quiet but profound transformation of the whole social and economic structure of the country. *But Labour will only remain in power if it succeeds in capturing the people's imagination.* They voted Labour because they were fed up with

31

the Tories; after five years of Virtue and Gloom, they may turn Stalinite or back to the Tories, for the same negative reasons. Gradualism and long-term planning are no justification for the fact that the *Daily Herald* is the drabbest and dullest paper in this country. If it can't change its editorial traditions, why can't the victorious Labour Party find the means to start a new, truly popular paper and get the politically indifferent masses away from the influence of the Rothermeres and Beaverbrooks and Kemsleys? The best journalists in this country are on the Left; but they have to work for the *Mail* and *Express* because there is no scope for them on a socialist paper in socialist Britain. Why can't socialist Britain produce films on the lives of Marx, or Robert Owen, or Keir Hardy, or the Tolpuddle Martyrs—which would be just as exciting as films on Henry VIII or Lady Hamilton? Why has the British working-class family to spend its holidays at home, or on a miserable excursion which consists mainly of queueing—for the train, for a room, for tea, lunch, cigarettes, cinemas—whereas Mr. Butlin's private holiday-camps for the lower middle classes are a roaring success, with sport, dances, entertainments and no end of fun for very little money? Why can't the Government hire Mr. Butlin—or study the Nazis' "Strength through Joy" organisation, which was in many respects a truly admirable thing? Why is the only place in any English village or town where a soldier can play billiards, read magazines, hear lectures and get cheap meals, the Y.M.C.A.—and why are Labour clubs the most cheerless places anywhere? Why is no serious attempt being made to show the people in this country what socialism is really about? We hear the news at nine o'clock; but where, to quote Eliot, where are the eagles and the trumpets?

The answer to these questions is, firstly, that each national branch of the working-class movement is bound to adapt itself to certain national characteristics. The ruthlessness of the Bolsheviks reflected the mentality of a semi-Asiatic country; the arduous theorists of the S.P.D. were steeped in German pedantry; the great tribunes of French socialism drew on the sources of latin eloquence; and the Labour Movement has inherited the Briton's proverbial main virtue and vice, his Lack of Imagination. (Lack of imagination has always been associated in this country with straightforwardness, reliability and tradition; its opposites, "smartness" and "cleverness", with dubious and mainly foreign practices.)

Furthermore, each political organism develops, as it advances in age, a kind of automatic filter system through the meshes of which only those are able to ascend to leadership who, in mentality and temperament, conform, by and large, to the required standard type; it is the equivalent of Natural Selection in the political field. Hence the prevalence in the British Labour Movement of the Transport House bureaucrat, and its contempt for "intellectuals" like Laski and Strachey, for brilliant *enfants terribles* like Nye Bevan, for people who are considered too clever by half like Crossman or too passionately sincere like Michael Foot. I could continue the list; if the outsiders were insiders, Britain could have the most dynamic Government in its history.

Another paradoxical aspect of the situation is that the forerunners of the political Labour movement, the Trade Unions, have to-day become the heaviest drag on the Labour Government. While I am writing this, the London transport workers are out on an unauthorised strike, and the socialist Government has had to resort to the ominous measure of calling in the Army to maintain London's food supply. Although the troops are being used to get the goods to the people and not to break the strike, the workers are of course unimpressed by such subtle distinctions; so bitterness is mounting, and the Government's stock is falling. Now even Conservative papers admit that the men's demands are reasonable enough—the main point being the reduction of the lorry-drivers' working week from 48 to 44 hours. The Transport and General Workers' Union, to which the men belong, backs their claims. It is the most powerful Union in the country. If it cannot reach agreement with the employers through the national joint negotiating machinery, it can ask for a committee of inquiry, appeal to Parliament, and so on. But the Union leaders in charge have let the negotiations drag on *for nine months*—on points of dispute which could have been settled in nine days. They "do not seem to have worried over the time wasted. They were unaware of the fact that the patience of the men was at an end. The leaders of this mammoth Union were clearly out of touch with the men they were supposed to represent. They seemed to know next to nothing of the mood of their members. So great is the gulf that has developed between the central executive and the rank and file, that both have come to obey different impulses . . . "

The above comment is from *Tribune*, the Labour weekly; I quote it to show you how generally it is realised among clear-sighted Labour politicians that the Trade Unions have become the most awkward problem of the socialist future. For it is almost mathematically predictable that as nationalisation and planning progress, and as the Unions become more and more absorbed into semi-governmental, managerial functions, the estrangement between their bureaucracy and the working masses will become even greater. The article ends with the pious hope that the Union leaders will regain the confidence of the rank and file. But it is an illogical hope. When the State becomes the biggest employer and the Unions part of the State bureaucracy, they cease to be an instrument of the working class and become an instrument for the coercion of the working class. That is what has happened in Russia, where the worker is once more as helpless as he was in pre-Tolpuddle days. *Who is going to protect the workers in the Workers' State?* The question is less paradoxical than it sounds, and I have found no answer to it in Labour's blueprints of the future. So that's another one for your symposium.

Land of Virtue and Gloom

I have no space left to talk about foreign policy; that will have to wait until the next Letter. As for outstanding literary events, they don't have to wait—there haven't been any.

London, June, 1947

DEAR EDITORS,

I am beginning to think that it was a mistake on your part to ask an ex-journalist turned novelist to write this London Letter. The present letter, for example, should have for its main theme the latest storm in a tea-cup caused by the Labour Rebels; the retort of the Executive; and some intelligent comment on the annual Labour Party Conference at Margate. But I am unable to defend myself against a desperate feeling of the futility and irrelevance of all this; against the conviction that whatever is said at Margate, or at UNO and UNESCO, has damned little to do with the fate of this country and the world in general. Once, in the prison of Seville, I overheard two guards arguing about whether a condemned man who had fallen ill with appendicitis should be given a milk diet while waiting for his execution; that is the feeling of nightmare against which I am battling in vain.

It seems that, just as certain paradoxes of logical reasoning cannot be solved, there are paradoxes of political reasoning equally insoluble. In the normal course of life, moral dilemmas occur in such a diluted state that, helped by habit and convention, we do not even realise having made an implicit choice. But in the decisive moments in the history of individuals and nations, the dilemma presents itself in an undiluted and explicit form.

If the British Isles could be cut loose from their continental moorings and ferried, say, into the Caribbean Sea, the choice would be easy. As it is, the memories of the Blitz, of V-1 and V-2 don't make the prospect of becoming America's aircraft-carrier or atom-bomb absorber particularly enticing. As *The New*

Statesman put it with its inimitable *naïveté*: "Our only hope is that by atomic neutrality we should avoid provoking either side to destroy us as an arsenal or as a base." Logically, this hope is of course moonshine, as the record of Belgian neutrality in two wars, the example of Holland and Norway, of Finland, of the Baltic and Balkan countries, proves. But if you happen to be an Englishman with a family and a house and a garden, you will naturally cling, against logic and reason, to the hope of getting somehow out of the necessity of taking sides. You will remember that England as a target is twenty miles from the Continent, but three thousand miles from America. Your cunning subconscious may even whisper to you that in the case of your benevolent neutrality toward Russia, the Americans would hesitate to let loose atom bombs or radio-active clouds against these islands, whereas in the opposite case the Russians would not hesitate to do so. And finally, people here have been told for six years what nice chaps the Russians are, and that Eastern democracy is only just a shade different from ours; so what's it all about anyway, and why get mixed up in other peoples' quarrels?

I suppose this is a rather depressing letter. Its aim was not to propose solutions, but merely to point once more to a curious characteristic of our time: that the most dangerous propagators of vileness and mental corruption are neither cynics nor terrorists with bombs—but men of goodwill, with strong frustrations and feeble brains: the wishful thinkers and idealistic moral cowards, the fellow-travellers of the death train. Like a swarm of gentle rodents, they are gnawing, gnawing away at the roots in the scorched fields.

London, October, 1947

DEAR EDITORS,

Only an exceptional imaginative effort could enable the Labour Government to win the next election. The future depends on its ability to stimulate the people's political consciousness and joy of life. Instead of which, they get "Work or Want" posters, unctuous sermons, and the death-sentence on the motor-bike through the abolition of the basic petrol ration.

> *The Cabinet takes Britain in its keeping*
> *In working partnership with sons of toil,*
> *But there's the rub—those partners now are sleeping,*
> *The revolution has gone off the boil,*
> *The plebs have lost that hectic joie-de-vivre*
> *That goes with revolutionary fever.*★

Two more years of this, and Labour will have irretrievably wasted its historic chance, and will have gone the way of the German, Austrian, and French social-democratic parties.

The fatal pattern of the Continental precedents is equally discernible in Labour's attitude towards the upper and the middle classes. The Weimar Republic had sufficiently scared the Junkers and the Ruhr industrialists to make them her mortal enemies; it kept on provoking them with pinpricks, but forgot to break the backbone of their power. Much the same happened in Austria, and in the France of the "Popular Front" era. With local variations it is always the same distressing spectacle. The young matador enters the arena, bows to the enthusiastic crowds, flaunts his red cape before the bull until the beast gets raving mad; then, in the decisive moment, it appears that he has left his sword at home, and he is carried out on a stretcher, past the booing spectators who throw cushions and rotten eggs at him.

In other words, a Socialist government cannot escape the fatal choice either of breaking the power of the old ruling classes, or of coming to a *modus vivendi* with them. Every single social-democratic movement in Europe since 1918 has tried to evade

★ From Sagittarius' brilliant political satire : *Let Cowards Flinch*, London, 1947.

this choice, and each has fallen a victim to its attempt at evasion. In this respect, the predicament of British Labour is merely an example of the predicament of democratic socialism in general, and the muddled policy of the Government may be regarded partly as a consequence of the inadequacy and datedness of socialist doctrine itself. But no such excuse can be claimed for the treatment of the storekeeper, artisan, small businessman, white-collar worker. The requirements of socialist policy towards this amorphous, politically opportunist mass, with its decisive influence on the climate of public opinion, and its decisive "floating vote", are clear and unambiguous: they must be won over to the side of the People, to which they belong. Experience both on the Continent and in this country has proved that the industrial working class alone, without middle-class support, can neither obtain a stable parliamentary majority, nor the necessary favourable *ambiance* of the street; it cannot govern.

To all this the staunch Labour supporter will answer that the Government has no choice, that all its actions are rigidly determined by Tory mismanagement in the past, by the dollar shortage and the export gap. It would be foolish to deny the extremely heavy economic odds against which the Government is battling; it is equally foolish and irresponsible to use facts, which were just as well known in 1945 when Labour fought its electoral campaign, to justify the ineptitude of, say, Shinwell's fuel policy last winter, or the symbolic lunacy of the abolition of motoring, or Bevin's running amok on Palestine. In my first letter to you I tried to show that this Government, like any other, had a wide elbow-room of subjective freedom for manœuvring within the hard limits set by objective conditions; and that goes for all fields of activity, from economics to public relations. At that time I said that after eighteen months of Labour rule it was too early to draw conclusions. To-day, in the third year of the régime, it is becoming clear that it is squandering at a rapid pace the goodwill of the electorate, the benevolent neutrality of the Little Man, and the sympathy and hopes of the European Left. If, within the next year, the Labour movement still retains sufficient vitality to change its leadership, both in spirit and in body, the downhill trend may still be halted; if not, 1950 will see the Conservative Party, perhaps reinforced by a few neo-Macdonaldites, reinstated in power. The British Labour victory was the last chance of the social-democratic movement in our time; if it is lost, it means that a Tory England allied to a Gaullist France will, for better or worse, tackle the European problem which socialism has been unable to solve.

Land of Bread and Wine *

1

ON 1ST JULY, 1947, *Sondage*, the excellent fortnightly bulletin of the French Institute of Public Opinion, published the results of a Gallup Poll on the question: "Do you believe that at the present moment things are going well or badly with France?" The answers were: Going well: 0 per cent. Rather well: 4 per cent. Badly, or rather badly: 93 per cent. No opinion: 3 per cent.

The near-unanimity of the answers shows that the series of convulsions which constitute French post-war history are not a surface disturbance, but rather the result of what is called here a *lame de fond*, a ground-swell which affects all the basic values of life.

Now the paradox about this profound upheaval is that apparently it cannot be traced to objective causes. Unlike England, France has emerged from the war with a temporarily weakened, but structurally intact and essentially sound economy. Unlike Germany or Italy, whose tragedies follow the classic pattern of defeat, France is in the camp of the victors. Unlike Poland or Rumania, she has no expanding Power of superior strength leaning over her frontiers. To put it crudely, the French seem to have no excuse for the frightening mess into which they have got themselves.

* Condensed version of two articles first published in *The Observer*, February, 1948.

Land of Bread and Wine

Just as the storming of the Bastille was not a local French event, but the symbol of the collapse of the feudal system in Europe, so the present situation in France is like a dramatisation on the stage of all the relevant contradictions and conflicts of the post-liberal era, which in more conservative or politically less sensitive nations are still in a stage of latency. This has happened before—in 1789, in 1848 and in 1871; it is the glory and tragedy of French genius, to serve as a burning lens of Western civilisation.

A central feature of the French crisis is the world-wide problem how to integrate farming communities, whose mental climate is, at the best, that of the nineteenth century, into the controlled economies of the twentieth. The Russian peasants in 1930 resisted the intrusion of the State by burning their crops and killing their cattle; the French farmer of to-day resists State control by turning his grain into pig-food instead of bread. The Russian State tried to break the resistance of the peasants by deporting five million to Siberia and terrorising the rest; the French, less single-minded, have to resort to the absurd expedient of importing foodstuffs which abound in the farms but never reach the market.

In all details the two processes are different; in their essence they represent developments parallel to each other and to developments in other parts of the world where peasant populations fight their stubborn rearguard actions against the planning and controls imposed by the industrial age. The French crisis, which began about two decades ago and was merely accelerated by the war, reflects the transformation of the last great bread-and-wine producing country of Western Europe.

The vicious spiral of wages and prices; the black, or rather grey market which, mainly based on direct barter between the urban population and their farming relatives, is to some extent a common-sense corrective to abstract planning; and a great number of other secondary factors of great complexity, are reducible either to this basic process or to factors other than economic. The present crisis was no more "caused" by war-inflicted losses in capital substance than the crisis of 1789 was "caused" by the salt-tax or the extravaganzas of the Court; it marks the end of an era in European economy in a typically French dramatised version.

If this diagnosis is correct, the crisis can be eased by foreign aid and other palliatives, but it cannot be solved within the framework of French economy alone. A plan of reconstruction as a self-contained economic unit is no more possible for France than for Wales or California, at least for the basic trinity of coal, steel, and cereals; blueprints for a French recovery can only make sense within the framework of Western Europe, including Western Germany, as an economically integrated unit.

2

The French situation reflects yet another general European trend over the past twenty-five years: the disgust with party-politics, the crisis of the parliamentary system, a certain anti-democratic nostalgia of the masses, and the division into two extreme opposing "blocks" which grind the softer mass between like millstones.

The Communists to-day present the same dilemma to France as the Nazis did to Germany in 1930. Should democratic privileges be extended to a party which aims at the destruction of democratic privileges? The dilemma is complicated by the fact that, while Nazism frankly professed its intention to abolish democracy, the Communists pose as its defenders. Their disfranchisement could be justified only by circumstantial evidence; once embarked on this course, democracy would deny its own principles and become absurd. The farcical proceedings in the French Chamber thus again merely reflect the more profound European dilemma. A political system which crystallised in the liberal era becomes increasingly inapplicable in the epoch of quasi-mystical mass movements led from abroad by remote-control switches, and liable at any moment to scuttle the nation.

As the remote switchboard of the Cominform permits all national extensions to display a certain amount of local colour, the successive transformations of the French Communist Party have been more picturesque than in any other country. A few months ago it still posed as the party of the Little Man, of bourgeois respectability and even sentimental jingoism. Its posters in the provinces told the farmers: "For the Defence of Property— vote Communist." Next came a brusque, ultra-revolutionary turning to strike, sabotage, and terror.★ As a result, the chances of civil war are discussed to-day in France in the same tone of voice as the possibilities of a new cut in the bacon ration in England.

In this respect again, what appears as a French internal crisis is in fact a function of the world crisis: for three centuries in succession, France has maintained its unenviable position as the centre in which the chronic stresses of Europe become acute. In retrospect, the country looks like a luminous canvas with fluid contours and coloured shadows, where all the major themes of our age are represented in the impressionist style, from the problems of the farming community to the collapse of ethical values. If France goes, Europe is gone, and this the French know; on the other hand France can only be saved as an integral part of Western Europe— and this they have so far refused to accept.

★ The wave of strikes and riots during the winter of 1947–8 brought certain areas of France to the verge of civil war.

The Candles of Truth*

A FORMER comrade of my Communist days asked me recently with an ironic smile what would be done to members of the Communist Party if I had my say. I told him that I would condemn them all to one year of Forced Reading. The sentence would start with a course in Russian to enable the offender to read Russian newspapers and listen to the Soviet radio. He would have to read *Pravda, Izvestia,* and *Komsomolskaya Pravda,* one social-economic magazine and one literary magazine, day by day, column by column. Then the collected speeches of the leaders, both living and dead, and the confessions of the dead before they died; then the school books, a selection of average magazine short stories, and patriotic poetry. The course would be confined to reading matter authorised by the Soviet Government, and all counter-revolutionary literature would be banned, including, of course, all newspapers, periodicals and books published in the capitalist world. It is my conviction, based on experience at the *locus in quo,* that, before the year was over, this enforced exposure of and to Soviet reality would act as a complete cure. Evidence are the few thousand foreign workers—mainly Austrian *Schutz-bund* people and German Communists—who were admitted into Soviet Russia. Unfortunately, their sentence did not come to an end after one year of forced reading of reality; theirs was a more drastic fate.

The facts of Soviet reality speak for themselves and constitute

* From the foreword to *Stalin's Russia,* by Suzanne Labin (London, 1949).

44

such an overwhelming indictment of the régime that, once they are known, comments can be dispensed with. The main difficulty is to get at the facts and to put them before the public. To get at them is difficult because of the double barrier of language and frontiers. To put them before the public is difficult because the facts are systematically drowned by floods of defamation and slander. The result is that the average Western European knows no more about the realities of everyday life in Soviet Russia than his forbears knew about China in Marco Polo's time.

Ignorance breeds illusions, and illusion, both of the positive and negative kind, is a mortal danger in politics. Soviet sympathisers contend that the existence of forced labour battalions, numbering approximately 10 per cent. of the total Soviet population, is a counter-revolutionary illusion. What better service could be done to the Soviet case, what more crushing defeat inflicted upon the literary hirelings of the imperialistic war-mongers, than to invite a trade union delegation to tour the Arctic, Siberian and Central Asiatic territories in which the alleged forced labour camps are located? To forestall accusations of bias, the delegation should include Soviet sympathisers of such undoubted sincerity as Professors Haldane and Bernal, Mr. Zilliacus and the Dean of Canterbury. If these men were given unrestricted freedom of movement and inquiry to enable them to check their beliefs against reality, I for one would accept their evidence, and so would a considerable section of British public opinion.

Positive illusions are no less dangerous than negative ones. The French and Italian Communists' acceptance of a policy deliberately aimed at wrecking European recovery is only made psychologically possible by their illusions about the structure and aims of the Soviet régime. Moreover, the existence of these strong Communist parties in various European and Asiatic countries, who in case of armed conflict are expected to side with the Red Army, is a potent inducement to the Soviets to continue their policy of expansion, and thereby to increase the risks of a third world war. Without the hope of support by civil wars, it would be suicidal for the Kremlin to challenge American military power; and the hope of civil war rests entirely on the masses of people whose addiction to the Soviet myth is based on their ignorance of reality.

It follows that if Soviet reality could be made accessible on a mass scale, the dangers of war would be considerably reduced. The myth-addict can only be cured by a shock-therapy of facts. What is needed is a Reader's Digest of the Soviet Press in English, French and Italian, featuring editorials, reports from the capitalist world, home news, literary criticism, all without comment; a monitored survey of Soviet home broadcasts, again without comment; popular editions in the Western European languages of the Soviet Labour Code, of Soviet electoral law and procedure, of Court procedure for dealing with political offences in public and in camera, of censorship regulations, of laws and administrative decrees regulating the Soviet citizen's rights to travel inside his country, to leave his place of residence, to apply for jobs and to leave jobs—all without comment; translations of Soviet first readers, extracts from Soviet textbooks of geography and history; a short booklet, exclusively based on translations from the Soviet Press and radio: "Europe through Russian eyes." What is needed above all is that our publishers and editors of the Left, who fed us for years on uncritical echoes of Soviet mythology, should awaken to their responsibilities. They have led the European public into a pink fog of half-truths. Their duty to-day is to help to dispel it before Europe suffocates, physically and morally; to dispel it, not by counter-propaganda and songs of hatred, but by the organised distribution of facts.

The world, tired of isms, its emotions burnt out, is thirsting for cold, clean facts. The torch of faith is extinct; let us fall back on the candles of truth.

The Seven Deadly Fallacies

Compressed version of an extempore lecture in
Carnegie Hall, New York, March, 1948

THE WAR hysteria from which a considerable number of people seem to suffer here in the United States is not a sign of mature awareness. Nor is the mentality of appeasement. Appeasement of an expanding power creates a fog in which neither of the opponents knows where he is; the aggressor, having grabbed positions A, B and C, hopes to get away with grabbing D—and why should he not hope so with all the encouragement that he receives from the opponent's camp? But position D—Poland in 1939, and maybe Italy to-day—has meanwhile come to be regarded by the other side as a *casus belli*, and so the world slides into war—without either of the opponents wanting it. Appeasement means playing poker; a firm, clearly outlined, principled policy means playing chess.

These are platitudes, the type of platitude which every reader of the *New Republic* or *The New Statesman and Nation* knew by heart in the 1930s. To-day they have forgotten it, and arguing against them means regressing to the kindergarten level. I hope that in this meeting we shall remain at least on the level of the primary school. So I shall take it for granted henceforth that war hysteria and appeasement are our Scylla and Charybdis, and that the liberal's precarious task is to navigate like Ulysses between the two.

47

The Challenge

Allow me, as an aid to navigation, to point out some of the logical fallacies and emotional eddies in which young idealists frequently get shipwrecked. I have listed for myself seven of them—the seven deadly fallacies of what you may allow me to call Left Babbittism. Here they are:

First is the *confusion of Left and East*. Some sections of the reactionary Press are unable or unwilling to distinguish between liberals, New Dealers, Social Democrats and Communists; they are all damned Reds. Naturally we are indignant at such poisonous imbecility. But the Left itself is partly responsible for this confusion. The Left Babbitt assumes that there is a continuous spectrum stretching from pale pink liberals to deeper red socialists and so on to purple Communists. It is time that he got it into his head that Moscow is not to his left but to his east. The Soviet Union is not a socialist country, and Cominform policy is not socialist policy. So let us bear in mind that "East is east and Left is left" and if the twain sometimes still meet, the meeting is purely coincidental.

The second fallacy is the *soul-searching fallacy*. The other day there was a press conference at which I mentioned that the frightened people in Italy and France look upon you Americans as their only hope of salvation, both from the economic point of view through E.R.P., and from the military point of view against open or disguised Russian aggression. Thereupon one of the reporters present said, "Do you really believe that we can help Europe with our dirty hands?" I asked: "What do you mean by 'dirty hands'?" He said: "Well, I mean our policy in Greece, and in Palestine, and backing up Franco, and the way we treat Negroes and Jews. We are dirty all over, and when we pose as defenders of democracy it is sheer hypocrisy."

The answer to this fallacy is to project the argument back to 1938. Then it would have run as follows: "We have no right to fight Hitler's plan of sending the Jews to the gas chambers so long

48

as there are 'restricted' hotels in America and so long as Negroes do not have absolute equality here. Once American democracy has become a perfect democracy, then and then only shall we have a right to defend what remains of Europe. And if Europe goes to the dogs before we have finished, that's just too bad and cannot be helped."

Third, and closely related to the soul-searching fallacy, is *the fallacy of the false equation*. Its European version runs: "Soviet totalitarianism is bad. American imperialism is equally bad. There is nothing to choose between them, so let us stay in No Man's land until fate catches up with us." To prove that the American system is "just as bad" as the Russian system, to make the two sides of the equation balance, your purist has recourse to half-conscious little subterfuges. He equates the Hollywood purges with the Moscow purges. He has never lived under a totalitarian régime, so when he draws comparisons he does not know what he is talking about. His conscience is in revolt against the appalling slums of Chicago, in which the Negro workers of the slaughter-house industry live like rats. I have spent a few days in Chicago, and I was appalled by what I saw and heard and smelled. Do not think I am a naïve tourist, a romantic admirer of your system. But now compare your treatment of racial minorities at its worst, with the Soviet treatment of the minorities of the Crimean Republic, the Chechen Republic, the Volga-German Republic, whose total populations were deported because they had, as the official Soviet communiqué said, "proved themselves unreliable during the war". Even the babes in their cradles were unreliable and had to go to Siberia. In Chicago I saw men on strike, and sympathised with them. In Russia strikes, or incitement to strike, are qualified as high treason and punished by the maximum penalty. In American elections political machines corrupt and distort the People's will. In Russian elections $99\frac{1}{2}$ per cent. vote for the one official list—the remaining $\frac{1}{2}$ per cent. presumably being in bed with influenza. Your enlightened Babbitt equates an imperfect democracy with a perfect totalitarian régime; his philosophy boils down to the maxim that there is nothing to choose between measles and leprosy.

Fallacy number four is the *anti-anti attitude*. It runs: "I am not a Communist. In fact, I dislike Communist politics, but I don't want to be identified with anti-Communist witch-hunting. Hence I am neither a Communist nor an anti-Communist, but an anti-anti-Communist. If W. R. Hearst says that twice two is four, I shall automatically hold that twice two is five, or at least $4\frac{1}{2}$." The $2 \times 2 = 4\frac{1}{2}$ mathematicians are usually Henry Wallace voters.

Don't laugh, for the roots of this fallacy are very deep in all of us, myself included. I remember how painful it was when a doddering elder in a London club walked up to me and said with a tap on my shoulder: "Well, young man, I am glad that at last you have come round to see reason. I myself knew twenty-five years ago what Bolshevism means, and it's never too late to repent."

You can't help this sort of thing; you can't help people being right for the wrong reasons. In the last war we fought in the name of democracy in an alliance with Dictator Metaxas of Greece, Dictator Chiang Kai-shek and Dictator Stalin. At that time Nazism was the main menace to the world, and politics is based on forming alliances. But there is a fundamental difference between a war-time alliance, and political identification with one's allies. Being allied to Chiang did not mean that we wished to imitate the Chinese régime. Being against our will in one camp with the Hearst press or Senator McCarthy does not mean that we identify ourselves with their ideas and methods. This fear of finding oneself in bad company is not an expression of political purity; it is an expression of a lack of self-confidence. If you are sure of yourself—politically and ideologically—you will no longer be frightened to say that twice two makes four, even if Colonel McCormick says the same.

Fallacy number five is *the sentimental fallacy*. For years we were allied to Communists in the struggle against Nazism, and now when we have to part company, the roots of past loyalty are difficult to tear out. Our bedfellows of yesterday do not share this sentimental squeamishness. Over the slightest disagreement they will denounce us as Fascists, traitors and cannibals. These emotional ties are one-way ties, and it is essential to bear in mind that they are entirely irrational and conservative in nature.

Fallacy number six is *the fallacy of the perfect cause*. It is related to number two, the soul-searching fallacy. Only absolutely clean hands have a right to reach out to protect and save what remains of Europe. Only an absolutely perfect cause is worth fighting for. And the search for the perfect cause becomes an excuse for quietism.

History knows no perfect causes, no situation of white against black. Eastern totalitarianism is black; its victory would mean the end of our civilisation. Western democracy is not white but grey. To live, even to die for a perfect cause is a luxury permitted to few. In 1942 or '43 I published an article which began with the words: "In this war we are fighting a total lie in the name of a half-truth." The total lie was Hitler's New Order. The half-truth was our democracy. To-day we face a similar emergency and a similar predicament. Once more the choice before us is merely that between a grey twilight and total darkness. But ask the refugees who manage to escape, at the risk of their lives, from behind the iron curtain into our grey twilight world whether this choice is worth fighting for. They know. You don't.

The last fallacy, number seven, is the *confusion between short-term and long-term aims*. It is the most dangerous of all. By long-term aims I mean the age-old struggle for reform, for social justice, for a more equitable system of government. By

51

short-term aims I mean the necessity of fighting an immediate emergency.

The danger of confusion is twofold. Your leftist Babbitt may refuse to fight against the short-term emergency until he has finished the job of creating a perfect government in his country, in a century or two. The opposite danger is to become so obsessed with the immediate emergency, that all principles of the long-term struggle are thrown overboard. Ex-Communists and disappointed radicals are in particular danger of toppling over to the other extreme. It is essential that we should keep in mind that there are two distinct levels involved in our struggle; that to defend our system against a deadly threat does not imply acceptance of everything in this system, does not imply giving up the long-term fight to improve it; and *vice versa*, that our criticism of the shortcomings of this system does not free us from the duty to defend it, despite its ambiguous greyness, against the total corruption of the human ideal.

This talk was mainly addressed to the progressive Left. I may have been harsh to the Left Babbitt; it was a brotherly harshness. To the Babbitt of the Right I have nothing to say; we have no language in common.

The power-vacuum which two world wars have created in Central and Western Europe, has inescapably linked your fate with that of the European continent. I feel the enormous burden which is falling on your shoulders. For there will either be a *Pax Americana* in the world, or there will be no pax. Never has such a burden and such a responsibility been borne by any single nation in history. It is the more unfair to you as yours is an adolescent civilisation, with adolescent enthusiasms and adolescent pimples. The task of the progressive intelligentsia of your country is to help the rest of the nation to face its enormous responsibilities. It is time for the American liberal to grow up.

Chambers, The Villain*

THE SECOND trial of Alger Hiss happened to coincide with the publication of a book in which several former Communists and Soviet sympathisers, including myself, relate their experiences. This explains the letter from which the following extract is taken. The writer is unknown to me—she is a woman, obviously of German origin, who now lives in a Latin-American country.

DEAR MR. KOESTLER,

In the *Time* issue of January 9th, Latin American Edition, where the book *The God That Failed* and your account in it, is mentioned, there appears, once again, a piece on the Alger Hiss trial.

Many were the times when I wanted to write to you. Many were also the times when I wanted to write either to Alger Hiss or to *Time* when I read again and again of that ominous trial, to express my sympathy and/or to cry out: isn't there anybody who is interested to present the case of Hiss in the right light of psychology and human understanding? I didn't do that either, because I thought who cares if I write or not.

Still, to-day I write to you because it came to me in a flash that it is you who really should write that letter which would be nothing if it came from a nobody like me, but if it comes from you it will be a plea that will be heard.

* First published in abridged form in *The New York Times*, February, 1950.

Reading about Alger Hiss I always think: there but for the grace of God and the Communist Party, stand I. I belong to your generation, in age and in spirit; I was one of those who, had the party only asked for it, would have spied on God Almighty without the least bit of a bad conscience. It is not my merit that they did never ask me things like that, because the only function I ever held was that of a dumb cashier of party dues, and later on I was fortunately only a no-account typist in one of their organisations in Berlin; still later, in Spain the same in a party office in Barcelona during the Civil War. It was around that time, summer 1937, when I changed my mind about our 'Religion' and no doubt, had Alger Hiss gone through this school he would have changed his mind also. But Americans were rather a few years later in finding out, you know the political reasons for that very well, I suppose. It seems one has to be a European with a left-wing past to understand the Hiss story . . .

That is where the call for you comes in. Defend Alger Hiss on ground of his motives. I only know of the Hiss case what I have read in *Time*. Still, the story seems in a way very clear to me and though I believe he did what he is accused of, I see it in the light of his then decent motives. The question would rather be: have the United States really been harmed through him? I cannot believe that. It must be his difficult position and regard for his family that makes him insist on his 'innocence' which, in a higher sense, is real. Come to think of it, for the American public the case is really a bit involved, but you could make it clear. Maybe, if you did, you would prevent a suicide. Could not this trial be brought around to the real issue: even if he did steal the documents, what were his motives? Probably, sometime between now and then, when Alger Hiss changed his mind as so many did who had been communists in good faith, he was in no position to announce that change. It must have been like this and Whittacker Chambers is the real villain because he didn't keep his mouth shut about things past and done with."

I have quoted this long extract because I believe that it expresses, in an admittedly exaggerated and overstrung manner, the vague feeling of uneasiness in a considerable section of the European and American public. The outstanding aspect of the trial was that it was not a case of the State calling a citizen to account for an alleged crime. It was a public and deathly duel between two individuals, one persecutor, one persecuted. Thus, the abstract equation of justice between individual and society became transformed into a personal equation between two men, and the whole picture became distorted by the public's emotional reactions to these two so utterly different human types. As far as personal impressions and the testimonies of high-standing witnesses go, the persecuted Hiss appeared as the prototype of the decent, modest, hard-working, well-spoken, happily married, idealistic American liberal who, even if assumed to be guilty, could not be suspected of having acted for any base reason or for personal gain. His persecutor, on the other hand, appeared as a man who unblushingly admitted having committed perjury, travelled with forged passports, lived with mistresses under false names, and was described by some academic gentlemen as a psychopath. To put the whole matter in a nutshell: from the spectator's point of view the casting of the parts was wrong—Chambers should have got the part of Hiss and Hiss the part of Chambers.

But the roles were only apparently miscast. For there is a tragic consistence and deep symbolism in both characters. There are many who, without doubting the verdict of the jury, agree that Hiss's innocence is "in a higher sense real". For my part I am convinced that Hiss did what he did out of misguided idealism, and that he kept passing the documents to the spy-ring happily as a boy scout performing his one good deed every day. He is the classic type who becomes addicted to the Communist drug, and never finds his way back from the lost weekend in Utopia. We always feel unhappy if it becomes necessary to send a man to prison for something he did in subjective good faith, based on a profound conviction—though if this necessity were neglected civilisation would disintegrate.

Hiss persisted stubbornly in his error; Chambers confessed and recanted his past. One would think that this decisive fact should have tilted the balance of sympathy towards Chambers. Yet my correspondent excuses Hiss's impenitence by his "difficult position" and calls Chambers the "real villain" because "he did not keep his mouth shut". And here again she seems to lend a shrill voice to public sentiment. For though it is said that one repentant sinner causes more rejoicing in Heaven than ten righteous men, here on earth the public spectacle of the repentant sinner causes at best a feeling of embarrassment, at worst a feeling of revulsion. And there, I believe, is the core of the whole problem.

Some time ago at a New York cocktail party a lady journalist attacked me with some vehemence. She said that people who had once been Communists should shut up and retire to a monastery or a desert island, instead of going round "teaching other people lessons". She spoke with deep conviction, which expressed a widespread popular feeling: mankind's instinctive horror of the renegade.

This horror probably has its roots in the collective unconscious, in past loyalties to church, clan or tribe which, even if apparently buried, remain potent emotional forces. Even those who in principle agree that there are considerations which may force a man to override his loyalties, and who accept the ethical justification of a given act of renegation—even those feel æsthetically repelled by the spectacle of the act itself. People don't mind if you betray humanity in the name of some attractive cause; but if you betray your club or party, they will turn from you in contempt.

This leads us to the curious fact that in our society most people are in the habit of manipulating two mutually exclusive sets of ethical rules without being aware of the contradiction between them. The first is expressed by sayings like "my country, right or wrong", or "if the Party demands it I will spy on God Almighty Himself". The second demands that a man should have the courage to become a traitor, renegade, or apostate if the interests of humanity demand it. Some of the War Trials of the last years were good examples of the confusion created by the simultaneous application of these contradictory rules of ethical conduct. Even more startling is the example of France, where people were shot, imprisoned or sentenced to "national ignominy" for having obeyed the orders of their own legal government. If you feel contempt for the renegade Chamberses and Kravchenkos, then you should feel sympathy for the loyal Ribbentrops and Lavals; and *vice versa*, if you condemn people for having "collaborated" with a totalitarian régime, then you must acquit those who have deserted such a régime.

But even if in theory you agree with this, the deserter remains an unwelcome sight, and like Coriolanus he may exclaim:

> *A goodly house: the feast smells well: but I*
> *Appear not like a guest.*

For of the two co-existent and contradictory rules of ethical conduct the first, which demands unquestioning loyalty to some flag, social body or institution, is much older and deeper embedded in our unconscious psyche. This may be illustrated by comparing the public's attitude to a Catholic convert on the one hand, to an unfrocked priest on the other. Everybody, including hardened atheists, respects the convert; but even atheists are embarrassed by an unfrocked priest taking a girl out to a dance. Now, in fact, both are renegades who have repudiated their former convictions. But the convert has only deserted the amorphous mass of unbelievers who do not represent a social institution and have no flags, emblems or party cards; whereas the priest has deserted a church with powerful binding symbols.

Chambers and Kravchenko and the rest of us who have once borne allegiance to the "God that Failed", will always be looked upon somewhat as unfrocked priests. This would be without much interest if it merely concerned the few individuals in question. In this case the simplest solution for these would be to follow the lady journalist's advice and satisfy the demands of good taste by retiring to a desert island.

But if Chambers had followed this advice, his repentance would have become meaningless, for the public would never have learned certain facts which it was essential for it to learn. And the same is true of Kravchenko, and Barmine, and Silone and the others. My correspondent asks why they can't "keep their mouths shut about things past and done with"; and the public, repelled by this flood of renunciations, disclosures and ringing *mea culpa*'s, ask with a shudder the same question. The answer is, simply, that these things are neither "past" nor "done with". The essential data for the ideological and strategical defence of our civilisation could never have been assembled if these men had had the discretion and good taste to keep their mouths shut. For only those who have worked inside the totalitarian machine know its true character and are in a position to convey a comprehensive picture of it; and in this sense at least it is true that one repentant sinner is a more valuable asset than ten righteous men who have never swerved from the path of democratic virtue.

The decisive fact about Chambers is that he has performed a service of great social utility. Not all acts of social utility curry favour with the public, or make the man who performs them appear in a favourable light. But it is essential that these two value-judgments, the first of an objective, the second of an emotive character, should remain neatly separated; and that the emotional factor should not obscure political judgment or interfere with the discharge of justice. It is not to be expected that the public should like the runaway priest—even if the church from which he has run away happens to be devoted to worshipping the devil. It is not even important that it should believe in the purity, or otherwise, of his motives to quit. The public is entitled to feel attracted or repelled by him, but it is not entitled to let its bias interfere with its judgment: to talk of betrayal where loyalty would mean persistence in crime, and to defend the agents of an evil régime on the grounds that those who denounce it are no saints.

The Little Flirts
of St. Germain des Près[*]

"HE IS honest after all. All his betrayals are prompted by loyalty", somebody remarks in Manes Sperber's new novel.[**] The same perverse loyalty seems to have inspired the new *trahison des clercs*, the most recent betrayal of the French intelligentsia. It makes little difference whether it is expressed openly or in the veiled form of passive complicities and revealing silences. In the service of truth, the sins of omission are the most infamous ones.

"Neither Fascism nor anti-Fascism" was in 1939 the motto of the common-or-garden variety of betrayal. "Neither Communism nor anti-Communism" is the motto of betrayal by loyalty. Loyalty to what? Firstly, loyalty to an ideal, without the moral force to live up to it—unfulfilled yearnings have a kind of dusty immortality. Secondly, loyalty to the world of adolescence, the revolt against family and convention, the nausea of puberty,[***] translated into the idiom of the class struggle. Thirdly, loyalty to that urge for self-castigation, inherent in the artist's condition, which, among the intellectuals of the Left, expresses itself in an abject prostration before the "proletariat"—not, to be sure,

[*] First published in *Le Figaro Littéraire*, Paris, July, 1949 ; translated from the French.
[**] Manes Sperber : *Et Le Buisson Devint Cendre*, Calmann-Lévy, Paris, 1949. English translation : *The Burned Bramble*, London, 1951.
[***] Allusion to Jean-Paul Sartre's novel *La Nausée*.

before the real victim of social injustice, but before a legendary and apocryphal figure, half Messiah, half Buffalo Bill.

The Cominform created a semantic black market where ideological hooch is sold under counterfeit labels inviting us to buy Peace, Democracy, Freedom and Happiness, guaranteed best quality, at greatly reduced prices. The naïve and illiterate can hardly be blamed for buying the stuff and getting drunk on it; but when intellectuals, the connoisseurs of vintages and labels, permit themselves to be taken in, we can only explain this odd psychological phenomenon as treason through loyalty or loyalty to treason. It makes no difference to them that the labels are being changed every six months; the intellectuals' cold intoxications are more difficult to cure than the habit of opium. "For", to quote another of Sperber's heroes, "once you have swallowed a lie of that monstrous size, there is no limit, you will swallow anything."

If one wants to get out of this Black Mass of logics, one must have the courage to be pedantically explicit. So long as the supporters of the G.P.U. are called the extreme "Left", that word will have an odium attached to it. To admit any continuity between "moderate" and "extreme Left" means to accept complicity and shared guilt. When the followers of Stalin are transferred to the extreme right wing of the hemicycle in the Palais Bourbon where the friends of the late Hitler once sat—then and only then will the air on the left be clean again.

The fact that in the course of the last twenty years the Soviet régime has transformed itself into a government of the extreme Right according to all classic criteria—jingoism, imperialist expansion, police rule without *habeas corpus*, monopoly of the means of production concentrated in the hands of a corrupt and self-perpetuating oligarchy, oppression of the masses, suppression of all opposition, abolition of civil and intellectual liberties—this tragic fact is only understood in its full depth and significance by those who have lived through the experience with their heart, flesh and bones. The pink intellectuals of St. Germain des Près who were merely sunbathing under the rays of the specious illusion will never understand the whole truth. They can only understand a half or a quarter of it, because they have only given a half or a quarter of themselves. They are the semi-virgins of totalitarian flirtations; the Peeping Toms who watch History's debauches through a hole in the wall; the *tricoteuses*, diligently knitting their novels and editorials in the shadow of the Lubianka. And when we, fallen angels, out of a Paradise transformed into a dark and immense torture-chamber, try to tell them what it was like, the semi-virgins, who have never fallen from anywhere, look at us with their innocent, myopic little smile and explain to us that we exaggerate, that the fall must have shaken our nerves and that the best thing for us would be to take a rest and shut up. One answers them: "My poor friend, you would be among the first to be gagged, deported, liquidated." But of course, they explain, we know all that, revolutions are bound to be ruthless, you can't make an omelette without breaking eggs, and so on and so forth. Oh, you little masochists of the Age of Reason,* how you itch with impatience to be raped!

However, before that embarrassing incident happens to you, you ought nevertheless to read Sperber's novel. Because we shall not keep silent, and now a new voice has been added to ours, strong, pure and lucid. You will find in it the whole range of that experience which you have never lived, and also all the experiences which—God forbid—may be in store for you. I said "the whole range" because the author of this novel is Eastern European by origin, a psycho-analyst by profession, and was a Communist for ten years by passion and conviction; and because the action of the book is divided between Berlin, Vienna, Prague and a number of lost villages in Poland and Yugoslavia during the decisive

* See the previous footnote.

years 1930–38. In a word, this is the saga of the Comintern, and the first one, and therefore an important literary event.

The book has its artistic weaknesses, which I find the more excusable since they are the same as mine: the ideas in it are more important than the characters, and the situations are more real than the people who participate in them—especially if they are of the feminine gender. But it seems to me that, thank God, the critics and the public are to-day more indulgent of these faults than they were twenty-five years ago.★

In spite of its weaknesses, *Et Le Buisson Devint Cendre* is a work of exceptional depth and range; it reflects, like an image in a stream with trembling and fluid contours, the most extraordinary adventure of the human spirit since the Medieval Church. For it seems that at certain times—

"the need for absolute certainty transforms humanity into a sewer, transforms religion into Churches, and ideas into police truncheons. Our Josmar who is capable of resisting any danger would be unable to resist a minute without his absolute certitude. And that is why he and his like have corrupted and ruined the movement. I shall not refuse to come to our Josmar's aid if he needs it, but I shall do it reluctantly, for I am not inclined towards pity for the pitiless"

This is said by an old Professor of History, a patrician from Vienna, the last melancholy dinosaur of the Liberal era. He feels no charity for the uncharitable, but shows them tolerance nevertheless; he is only intolerant towards himself:

"At twenty, one ought to meet the inspiration of one's life, at thirty the woman of one's life, at forty one's private truth; at fifty one ought to have quenched one's thirst for

★ In France though not in England.

success, at sixty create a work greater than its creator, at seventy one ought to feel humble towards the humblest of one's contemporaries and arrogant towards the sky: I worked out this formula when I was twenty-five. Most people only discover their own design when they have failed to execute it. I discovered it so early that at every stage I knew in advance the exact time of departure of the train I was going to miss."

That personage, however, was born at a time when a man could still afford to miss his train with a smile. In the Europe of our day "only a lucky few will be awarded the benefit of a second warning". There was no second warning awarded to the countries in that part of the world from which Sperber and I come. Won't you learn from our experience, you clever little flirts of St. Germain des Près? Yes and No, they whisper. With them it is always Yes and No—or rather "Oh no, please don't". They neither want the Russians nor the Atlantic Pact. Neither capitulation nor self-defence. Neither life nor death. They are only happy doing a verbal pirouette on the tightrope over the No Man's Land, suspended between heaven and earth. And they will never understand that under Stalin and Thorez there will be no pirouettes, no neutrality, and No Man's Land.

But where is the morale, the message of hope which ought to be found at the end of every proper novel of the Left? There isn't much of it. Two fallen angels, one released from a German, the other from a Russian prison, sit side by side talking on a bench in the little square in front of Notre-Dame:

They didn't notice the first heavy drops, and the shower caught them unawares. They were alone on the square. The people who had taken refuge under porches watched with good-humoured amusement the two strangers getting soaked.

"When all is said, this kind of freedom has its good side", said Djoura. "In our part of the world, we couldn't remain sitting in the rain without attracting suspicion. Bourgeois democracy allows a man to be unhappy in his own fashion."

You think that for a message this isn't much of a message? Go and ask our friends in Siberia. You think that it is a renunciation of our revolutionary vows? There you are almost right. We have betrayed a party; you are only betraying humanity.

II
DIVERSIONS

An Anatomy of Snobbery

AN EARNEST essay on snobbery is an undertaking almost as humourless as an earnest essay on humour—which I have also done. But I have been fascinated by the subject for many years (particularly since I have settled in England), and I have gradually become convinced that snobbery is not merely a silly human weakness, but something basic in the mentality of modern man— a symptom which reflects the general sickness, the dislocation of social and cultural values in contemporary civilisation.

I shall talk of cultural snobbery first, of social snobbery later.

1

In the days before Hitler, the licentious days of the Weimar Republic, I knew in Berlin a young woman who worked for a left-wing publishing firm. Mary B. was attractive, clever, and notoriously promiscuous. There was a standing joke about her which asserted that she had slept with every author of the firm whose books sold more than twenty thousand copies; age and sex did not matter. As I had not yet written a book, I had obviously no chances with Mary, but we were friends, and one day I asked her whether the rumour was true. Mary said quite seriously that on the whole it was, and then explained the reason for what appeared to be an extreme case of literary snobbery.

She came from a very strict Lutheran family of the East

Prussian gentry. She had run away from home at twenty "to lead her own life". She had been attracted by a number of young men in succession, but found erotic pleasure frustrated by her intense awareness of sin. At twenty-one she was seduced by a famous writer who physically did not attract her at all, and to her surprise experienced the sensations which on previous occasions had eluded her, without any feeling of guilt. This incident was the beginning of her "twenty-thousand-and-over" complex.

The explanation of it she found herself. It took the form of an imaginary dialogue with her stern father:

" . . . But you see, Papa, having an affair with a famous man is not frivolous—it is like going to bed with History. Who would blame Marie Walewska for surrendering to Napoleon? Everything you do with a famous man is redeemed from its sinfulness by becoming a Historical Anecdote."

Mary perished as a victim of her complex. She became the mistress of Michael Kolzov, the once famous *Pravda* correspondent, an unattractive and insignificant-looking little man who was read not merely by twenty thousand but by two million people. During the great purge of 1938, Kolzov vanished, and Mary vanished with him. I shall come back to her later on, for I believe that her case will help to illuminate some of the more obscure aspects of the psychology of snobbery.

2

A friend of mine, whom I shall call Brenda, was given for her birthday by one of her admirers a Picasso line-drawing in a simple modern frame. It was an admirable and typical sample of Picasso's "classical" period: a Greek youth carrying a girl in his arms, the contours of the two figures somehow mixed up and partly indistinguishable like those of Siamese twins with shared limbs, yet adding up to a charming and harmonious total effect. It looked like a lithograph, but it bore no serial number, so Brenda took it to be a reproduction and hung it, somewhat disappointed with the gift, in her staircase. On my next visit, several weeks later, it was hanging over her drawing-room mantelpiece. "I see the Picasso reproduction has been promoted", I said. "Reproduction!" she cried indignantly. "It turned out it's an original! Isn't it lovely? Look at that line along the girl's hip . . . ", etcetera.

As a matter of fact, it was an original—a shyly understated gift of the mumbling and devoted admirer. But as it was a line-drawing in ink, consisting of nothing but black contour on white paper, it needed an expert, or at least a good magnifying lens to decide whether it was an original, a lithograph or a reproduction. Neither Brenda nor any of her visitors could tell the difference. Yet they took it for granted, as we all do, that an original deserves a proud display whereas a reproduction belongs, at best, on the staircase.

I shall now try to analyse, in a pedantic way, the reason for this attitude, apparently so natural. The original is, of course, many times more expensive than a reproduction; but we would indignantly reject the idea of displaying a picture simply because it is expensive; we pretend to be guided in these matters by purely æsthetic considerations. Next, one might surmise that our contempt for reproductions originates in the poor quality, and even poorer choice of subjects, of the Victorian print. But modern printing techniques have achieved miracles, and some Ganymede reproductions of aquarelles are almost indistinguishable from the original. In the extreme case of the line-drawing, we have complete æsthetic equivalence between original and reproduction.

And yet there is something revolting in this equivalence. It even takes a certain courage to admit to oneself that the æsthetic effect of a copy might be indistinguishable from that of the original. We live in an age of stereotyped mass-production; and after mass-produced furniture, mass-produced and prefabricated houses, the idea of mass-produced Piero della Francescas is indeed revolting. But we have no similar objection to mass-produced gramophone records; nor to mass-produced books, and yet they too fall into the category of "reproductions". Why then do you prefer, according to your income, a more or less second-rate original picture on the wall to a first-rate reproduction of a masterpiece? Would you rather read a mediocre young poet in manuscript than Shakespeare in a paper-cover edition?

Our argument seems to have become bogged down. Let us find out what Brenda herself has to say to explain her behaviour, in a dialogue with the writer:

Brenda: "I simply can't understand what all this fuss and talk is about. But *of course* my attitude to the drawing has changed since I knew that Picasso himself did it. That has nothing to do with snobbery—it's just that I wasn't told before."

K: "Your attitude has changed—but has that thing on the wall changed?"

B: "Of course it hasn't, but now I *see* it differently!"

K: "I would like to understand what it is that determines your attitude to a picture in general."

B: "Its quality, of course."

K: "And what determines its quality?"

B: "Oh, don't be such a pedant. Colour, composition, balance, harmony, power, what have you."

K: "So, in looking at a picture, you are guided by purely æsthetic value-judgments, depending on the qualities you mentioned?"

B: "Of course I am."

K: "Now as that picture hasn't changed, and its qualities haven't changed, how can your attitude have changed?"

B: "But I have told you before, you idiot. Of course my

attitude to it is now different, since I know it isn't one reproduction in a million, but done by Picasso himself. Can't you see?"

K: "No, I can't; you are contradicting yourself. The rarity of the object, and your knowledge of the manner in which it came into being do not alter the qualities of that object, and accordingly should not alter your judgment of it, if it were really based on purely æsthetic criteria—as you believe it to be. But it isn't. Your judgment is not based on what you *see*, but on a purely accidental bit of information, which might be right or wrong, and is entirely extraneous to the issue."

B: "Wrong! How *dare* you insinuate that my Picasso isn't an original? And how *dare* you say that the question whether he drew it himself is 'extraneous' to the issue?"

And so it will go on indefinitely. Yet Brenda is not stupid; she is merely confused in believing that her attitude to an object of art is determined by purely æsthetic considerations, whereas in fact it is decisively influenced by factors of a quite different order. She is unable to see her picture isolated from the context of her knowledge of its origin; and if she were to learn that it is after all a reproduction, her attitude would again change according to the changed context. Moreover, she is genuinely indignant at the suggestion that the question of its origin has nothing to do with æsthetic value as such. For, in our minds, the question of origin, authorship and authenticity, *though in itself extraneous to æsthetic value*, is so intimately and indistinguishably fused with our attitude to the object, that we find it well-nigh impossible to isolate the two. Thus Brenda unconsciously projects one scale of values onto a system of quite different values.

Is Brenda, then, a snob? It depends on the definition of snobbery at which we hope to arrive at the end. But as a working hypothesis, I would like to suggest that this process of unconsciously applying to any given field a judgment derived from an alien system of values, constitutes the essence of the phenomenon of snobbery. By these standards Brenda would *not* be a snob if she had said: "The reproduction in this case is just as beautiful as the original. But one gives me a greater thrill than the other for reasons which have nothing to do with beauty." She is an unconscious snob because she is unable to distinguish between the two elements of her experience, unable to name the extraneous cause of her biased æsthetic judgment, or to see that it *is* biased.

I am aware of labouring an apparently obvious point. But it will become at once less obvious if we turn to a different, yet related problem.

3

In 1948, a German art restorer named Dietrich Fey, engaged in reconstruction work on Lübeck's ancient St. Marien Church, stated that his workmen had discovered traces of Gothic wall-paintings dating back to the 13th century, under a coating of chalk on the church walls. The restoration of the paintings was entrusted to Fey's assistant, Lothar Malskat, who finished the job two years later. In 1950, Chancellor Adenauer presided over the ceremonies marking the completion of the restoration work in the presence of art experts from all parts of Europe. Their unanimous opinion, voiced by Chancellor Adenauer, was that the twenty-one 13th-century Gothic saints on the church walls were "a valuable treasure and a fabulous discovery of lost masterpieces".

None of the experts on that or any later occasion expressed doubt as to the authenticity of the frescoes. It was Herr Malskat himself who, two years later, disclosed the fraud. He presented himself on his own initiative at Lübeck police headquarters, where he stated that the frescoes were entirely his own work, undertaken by order of his boss, Herr Fey, and asked to be tried for forgery. The leading German art experts, however, stuck to their opinion: the frescoes, they said, were without doubt genuine, and Herr Malskat was merely seeking cheap publicity. An official Board of Investigation was appointed which came to the conclusion that the restoration of the wall-paintings was a hoax —but only after Herr Malskat had confessed that he had also manufactured hundreds of Rembrandts, Watteaus, Toulouse-Lautrecs, Picassos, Henri Rousseaus, Corots, Chagalls, Vlamincks and other masters, and sold them as originals—some of which were actually found by the police in Herr Fey's house. Without this *corpus delicti*, it is doubtful whether the German experts would ever have admitted having been fooled.

My point is not the fallibility of the experts. Herr Malskat's exploit is merely the most recent of a number of similarly successful hoaxes and forgeries—of which the most fabulous were probably van Megeeren's false Vermeers. The disturbing question which they raise is whether the Lübeck saints are less beautiful, and have ceased to be "a valuable treasure of masterpieces", simply because they had been painted by Herr Malskat and not by somebody else? And furthermore, if van Megeeren can paint Vermeers as good as Vermeer himself, why should they be taken off the walls of the Dutch and other National Galleries? If even the experts were unable to detect the difference, then surely the false Vermeers must procure as much æsthetic pleasure to the common run of Museum visitors as the authentic ones. All the curators would have to do is to change the name on the catalogue from Vermeer to van Megeeren.

There are several answers to this line of argument, but before going into them I want to continue in the part of *advocatus diaboli*, by considering an example of a forgery in a different field: Macpherson's *Ossian*. The case is so notorious that the facts need only be briefly mentioned. James Macpherson (1736-96), a Scottish poet and adventurer, alleged that in the course of his wanderings in the Highlands he had discovered some ancient

Gaelic manuscripts. Enthusiastic Scottish *littérateurs* put up a subscription to enable Macpherson to pursue his researches, and in 1761 he published *Fingal, an ancient Epic Poem in Six Books, together with several other poems composed by Ossian, the Son of Fingal.* Ossian is the legendary third-century hero and bard of Celtic literature. *Fingal* was soon followed by the publication of a still larger Ossianic epic called *Temora*, and this by a collected edition, *The Works of Ossian.* The authenticity of Macpherson's text was at once questioned in England, particularly by Dr. Johnson (whom Macpherson answered by sending him a challenge to a duel), and to his death Macpherson refused, under various unconvincing pretexts, to publish his alleged Gaelic originals. By the turn of the century the controversy was settled; it was established that while Macpherson had used fragments of ancient Celtic lore, most of the "Ossianic texts" were of his own making.

Yet here again the question arises whether the poetic quality of the work itself is altered by the fact that it was written not by Ossian the son of Fingal, but by James Macpherson? The "Ossianic" texts were translated into many languages, and had a considerable influence on the literature and cultural climate of Europe in the late eighteenth and early nineteenth century. This is how the *Encyclopedia Britannica* sums up its evaluation of Macpherson:

> "The varied sources of his work and its worthlessness as a transcript of actual Celtic poems do not alter the fact that he produced a work of art which . . . did more than any single work to bring about the romantic movement in European, and especially in German, literature. . . . Herder and Goethe . . . were among its profound admirers."

These examples could be continued indefinitely. Antique

furniture, Roman statuary, Greek tanagra figures and Italian madonnas are being forged, copied, counterfeited all the time, and the value we set on them is not determined by æsthetic appreciation and pleasure to the eye, but by the precarious and often uncertain judgment of experts. A mediocre but authenticated picture by a known master is held in higher esteem than an artistically superior work of his unknown pupil or "school"— not only by art dealers guided by "investment" but by all of us, including this writer. Are we, then, all snobs to whom a signature, an expert testimonial, or the postmark of a given period is more important than the intrinsic beauty of the object itself? And what about the contested works of Shakespeare and Johann Sebastian Bach? Are their dramatic and poetic and harmonic qualities dependent on the endless technical controversy between specialists and scholars?

4

I now propose to present the case for the defence. It can be summed up in a single sentence: our appraisal of any work of literature and art is never a unitary act, but the result of two independent and simultaneous processes which tend to distort each other.

When we look at an Egyptian fresco, we do not enjoy the painting at its face value, but by means of an unconscious re-attunement of the mind to the values of the period. We know, for instance, that the Egyptians had not discovered the technique of perspective in depth. We know that on certain Egyptian murals the size of the figures is determined by their relative social rank. Similarly, we look at every picture through a double frame: the solid frame which isolates it from its surroundings and creates for it a hole in space, as it were; and the unconscious frame of reference in our minds which creates for it a hole in time, and locates it in its period and cultural climate. Every time we think that we are making an æsthetic judgment based on pure sensory perception, we are in fact judging relative to this second frame or context or mental field.

Any work of art, or literature, or music, can only be appreciated against the background of its period, and that is what we unconsciously do; when we naïvely believe that we are applying absolute criteria, we are applying relative ones. When we contemplate the false Vermeer for the first time, believing it to be authentic, and the second time knowing that it is a fake, our æsthetic experience of it will in fact completely change, though the picture has remained the same. For it is now seen in a different frame of reference and therefore, in fact, differently. The same considerations apply to the perpetrator of the fake. He may be able to imitate the technique of the seventeenth-century Dutch School, but he could not spontaneously start painting like Vermeer—because his visual organisation is different, his perception of reality is different, and because he cannot, except by an artificial effort, erase from his mind the accumulated experience of everything that has happened in painting since Vermeer. And if, by a *tour de force,* a contemporary artist succeeded in reconditioning his own vision to that of the Dutch seventeenth-century or the Italian Quattrocento, he would have to use mass-hypnosis to recondition the vision of his customers in a similar manner.

We can add to our knowledge and experience, but we cannot subtract from it. When Picasso decides to disregard the laws of perspective, that means that he has passed through and beyond a certain technique—unlike the Egyptian painter, who has never acquired it. Evolution is an irreversible process; the culture of a period might apparently point in the same direction as an earlier one, but it does so from a different turn of the spiral. A modern primitive is different from a primitive primitive; contemporary classicism is different from any classical classicism; only the mentally insane are able to amputate part of their past.

And·yet when we contemplate works of the past, we must perform just such a process of mental subtraction, by attuning our minds to the climate and experience of the period. In order to appreciate them, we must enter into their spirit by forgetting our modern experience and all that we have learnt since that Homeric epic or Byzantine mosaic was created. We must descend into the past, making our mind a blank; and as we do so, we unconsciously condescend. We close our eyes to crudities of technique, naïveties of perception, prevailing superstitions, limitations of knowledge, factual errors. We make allowances. A little honest introspection will always reveal the element of condescension contained in our admiration for the classics; and part of our enjoyment, when listening to the voices of the past, is derived from this half-consciously patronising attitude—"how clever of them to know that at their age!" We feel that we have descended a turn of the spiral; we are looking up in awe and wonder at Dante's dreadful Paradise, but at the same time we seem to be bending down with a tender, antiquarian stoop.

This legitimate kind of æsthetic double-think degenerates into snobbery at the point where the frame of reference becomes more important than the picture, when the thrill derived from the gesture of bending over the past dominates the æsthetic experience. The result is a widespread confusion of critical judgment—overestimation of the dead and belittlement of the living, indiscriminate reverence for anything that is "classical", "antique", "primitive", or simply old. In its extreme form this tendency prompts people to have their wall-brackets and picture-frames artificially dirtied to lend them the patina of age; so let us call it the "patina-snobbery".

The process that leads to these distortions of judgment is basically the same as outlined before: the projection of one scale of values into a psychologically related but objectively alien field of experience. The essence of snobbery is to assess value according to a wrong type of scale; the snob is always trying to measure beauty with a thermometer or weight with a clock.

5

The thirteen-year-old daughter of a friend was recently taken to the Greenwich Museum. When she was asked which was the most beautiful thing she had seen in the Museum, she said unhesitatingly: "Nelson's shirt". When asked what was so beautiful about it, she explained: "That shirt with the blood on it was jolly nice. Fancy real blood on a real shirt, which belonged to somebody really historic!"

The child's thrill is obviously derived from the same source as the magic that emanates from Napoleon's inkpot, the lock of hair on the Egyptian mummy's head, the relic of the saint carried in annual procession, the strand of the rope by which a famous murderer was hanged, and from Tolstoi's laundry bill. In the mentality of primitive man, an object which had been in contact with a person is not merely a souvenir; it becomes magically imbued with the substance of that person, and in turn magically emanates something of that substance.

"There is, I am sure, for most of us, a special pleasure in sinking your teeth into a peach produced on the estate of an Earl who is related to the Royal Family", a columnist wrote recently in the *Daily Express.*★

Primitive magic survives in the subconscious; the strand of hair carried in the locket, grandmother's wedding-dress, the faded fan of the first ball, the regimental badge, all have a half-conscious fetish character. The bobby-soxers who tear shreds off

★ Quoted from "This England," *The New Statesman and Nation,* 14 August, 1954.

the crooner's garb are the vulgarised twentieth-century version
of the worshippers cherishing a splinter from the saint's bone.
The value we set on original manuscripts, on "signed" pieces
of furniture, on Dickens' quill and Galileo's telescope, is a more
dignified manifestation of the same unconscious tendency. It is,
as the child said, "jolly nice" to behold a fragment of a marble
by Praxiteles—even if it is battered out of human shape, with a
leper's nose and broken ears. The contact with the Master's hand
has imbued it with a magic quality which has lingered on and
radiates at us, conveying the same thrill as "the real blood on
Nelson's real shirt".

The change in our attitude—and in the art dealer's price—
when it is learnt that a cracked and blackened piece of canvas is
an "authenticated" work by X has nothing to do with beauty,
æsthetics or what have you—it is the working of sympathetic
magic in us. (See Brenda and her Picasso drawing.) The inordinate
importance that we attribute to the original, the authenticated,
in those borderline cases where only the expert could tell the
difference, is a derivative from primitive fetishism. And as every
honest art dealer will admit, these borderline cases are so frequent
as to be almost the rule. Moreover, it was in the past a general
practice for the master to let his pupils assist in the execution of
larger undertakings. To the majority of mortals, even those with
a discerning taste, the difference between an "authenticated"
masterpiece, an "attribution" and a "from the school of" is in
most cases not discernible. The brutal truth is that within most
periods and schools with a firmly established and conventionalised
style, the difference in quality between the competent practi-
tioners of that style is only relevant to those who specialise in that
epoch. It is not the eye that guides the average museum visitor,
but the magic of names and the magic of age. The bedevilment of
æsthetic experience by unconscious fetish worship and patina
snobbery is so general that it has become a major factor in our

attitude to the art of past epochs. It is an attitude as remote from spontaneous appreciation as the "Emperor's Clothes" approach to hyper-modern forms of art. The last mentioned aberration is too obvious to require discussing; and I shall now turn from cultural to social snobbery.

6

Prince Charles still has all his teeth. A rumour that he has lost one, set the crowds straining to see last night.

DAILY SKETCH, *October,* 1954

"Pends-toi, brave Crillon; nous avons combattu à Arques et tu n'y étais pas."★ I have forgotten what Crillon answered to Henry IV, but I am sure that he cursed himself for the rest of his life for having missed the historic opportunity. What I propose to call "the Crillon complex" may be loosely defined as the urge to participate in, or at least be present at, the making of History. At a first glance this may seem a peculiarity shared only by a few, the ambitious and the envious; but I believe that this urge is deeper than appears, and affects a large number of people in varying degrees.

Mary B. was an extreme example—in her case the Crillon complex took the form of wanting "to sleep with History". A less extreme form is the widespread desire to "meet" famous or historic personalities. Superficially it seems to be motivated by gross social vanity, by the urge to boast: "I have met the famous X". There may also be present a genuine curiosity to find out what X looks like "in real life". But the millions who used to flock to the White House to shake the President's hand before that custom was abolished, were driven not so much by vanity

★ "Hang yourself, brave Crillon ; we fought at Arques and you were not there."

or curiosity as by the desire to "shake hands with History". The crowds who go to any length of trouble to catch a glimpse of a coronation or a visiting statesman or the eruption of a volcano, are at least partly motivated by the desire to "have been present", to "witness history in the making", to participate, in whatever passive or remote manner, in the world-shaping events of one's time. The reverse of this urge is the fear of "missing something", of failing to exploit to the full the chance of being a contemporary, a witness of one's time.

The Crillon complex produces a rather touching variety of social snobs: the Peeping Toms of History, obsessed by the desire to "have been present", and to meet important people who, in one field or another, influence the destinies of their time. Boswell was perhaps the most outstanding historic snob, the prototype of all celebrity-hunters and autograph-collectors, of the people who will camp all night in the streets to catch a passing glimpse of some famous personality or event.

Social life is permeated with the Crillon complex, and our choice of company is profoundly influenced by it. We have a preference for people with some achievement to their credit which, however remote from our own interests, makes them "important" in their field; for people who are likely to leave their imprint on our time. Whether they leave their imprint as politicians, Chinese scholars, or collectors of snuff-boxes does not matter; nor do their human qualities. The value of people on the social market is determined not by what they are but by what they represent. To be oneself is not enough; one must be "somebody".

The phenomenon is so general that a society free from the germ of snobbery is difficult to imagine. In such an aseptic society, human beings would be judged by their intrinsic value and not by rank, fame, wealth, or professional achievement. But at once the question arises: what exactly do we mean by intrinsic value? Courage or humility, wit, or warmth, or saintliness? We cannot arrive at value-judgments without a frame of reference; appraisals can only be made by selecting a specific yardstick. We cannot even ask whether the yardstick is "appropriate" as such. A boxing fan is not a snob although he sets a higher value on Joe Louis than on T. S. Eliot; nor is the music enthusiast to whom Yehudi Menuhin is more important than Winston Churchill. Yet the social hostess with the musicality of a cow, who raves about Yehudi and longs to have him for a cocktail party, is a snob, because she pretends to measure value by one quality whereas in fact she measures it by another.

Under exceptional circumstances, a social group may acquire a "monolithic" hierarchy of values, and such groups are relatively free from snobbery, because there is no other scale of values to interfere with judgment. At the front line, or on a dangerous expedition, a combination of courage, optimism, skill and comradeship is the supreme value which temporarily excludes all other yardsticks, and lifts the individual out of his normal context of rank, social position, etc. "Closed" societies such as prison camps, sanatoria, monasteries, also tend to develop a monolithic system of values, though here the combination of qualities required is a different one. Under such conditions of extreme pressure, members of the closed group seem to judge each other purely by "intrinsic value" or "human quality" stripped of all considerations which normally bias judgment.

Under normal conditions, however, human society is a chaos of mutually exclusive systems of value which constantly intersect, overlap and clash. I have tried to show how in the appreciation of art, which we believe to be based on purely æsthetic criteria, alien systems interfere and turn us into cultural snobs. The tendencies which interfere with our appreciation of human qualities and turn us into social snobs are of a more obvious nature; the psychological roots of the worship of title, power, wealth, are easily traced. The difficulty here is to reach agreement on the question: which are the human qualities on which we think that our social preference *should* be based?

The answer can only be tentative and vague; yet by and large our confessed inclination would be to choose as friends people whose company we find both stimulating and relaxing, with whom we share certain tastes and interests, a cultural or social background, who are loyal and understanding and remain attractive human beings when stripped of all their distinction of rank or profession. In fact, however, the choice of the company we keep is guided by all these considerations to a lesser extent than we care to admit. The catch is in the purely fictitious assumption that we can ever strip a person of his background or "frame".

Let me take an obvious—and depressingly typical—example. At a crowded literary cocktail party I was introduced to a dull, middle-aged woman, who paid me some dull compliment about a book. As I had not been able to catch her name, I asked her whether she, too, wrote. "No", she said, "I am running a dress-maker's shop". I edged away at the first opportunity with a sigh of relief, and talked to somebody else, who then asked: "How did you like the Princess de G.?"—mentioning one of the great historic names of France. I turned and had another look at the dull woman—and, lo! how fascinating she had become. She had changed no more than the Picasso reproduction which had turned out to be an original, but my frame of reference had changed, making her appear in a different context and in a different light. Thus for instance, the fact that a descendant of those legendary figures was running a dress-maker's shop appeared significant in itself, and so did the terrible banality of her conversation. Ironically, further enquiry unearthed the fact that the Princess was a former mannequin, merely related by a short and episodic marriage to the house of G. This put her back into the original context; the Picasso was once more relegated to the staircase.

However, not more than two hundred years ago, my quick

changes of attitude would not have been considered snobbish at all, but a natural consequence of an accepted hierarchy of values, according to which a Princess in her own right naturally took precedence over a person of common origin. And the passionate interest in Prince Charles's teeth would have appeared as a perfectly normal and touching manifestation of the populace's devotion to their future king. The Europe of the feudal era had indeed a nearly monolithic hierarchy of social values in which birth, rank and station, appointed by the grace of God, provided a generally accepted yardstick. After the storming of the Bastille and the declaration of the Rights of Man, the system of values changed—at least theoretically. But the archetypal roots of the older values, and their symbols of noble kings and fair princesses, robber barons and chivalrous knights, have survived and constantly interfere with our liberal and democratic outlook. Pomp and circumstance, rank and consequence, title and lineage, have remained with us as a kind of psychological black-market currency under the social counter.

7

Every variety of the innumerable forms of snobbery can be traced back to the same basic pattern, the overlapping of two different systems of value. The first, S1, is the system on which we pretend or believe our judgments to be based: æsthetic criteria, personal attraction, intrinsic human qualities, and so on. The second, S2, is the interfering system which distorts our judgment: fetish-worship, "Crillon complex", title, power, and so on. To repeat, in a more precise form, the proposed definition: *snobbery is the result of the psychological fusion of two independent value-systems which are separate by origin and nature, but inextricably mixed up in the subject's mind.*

This does not mean that S2, the "interfering" system, is in itself worthless; its emotional power, which distorts the values of S1, is often derived from deep, archetypal sources. Only an inverted snob will pretend for instance that "the aristocracy", in the original sense of an élite formed by tradition and breeding, with the resulting high standards of comportment, manners and taste, is devoid of value. European culture, prior to the fall of the Bastille, was by and large feudal and aristocratic; the ambiguity of the term "common man" reflects the brutal fact that a lower social standard was synonymous with coarser manners and vulgarity of taste. In countries which have either undergone a thorough social revolution, such as France or Soviet Russia, or are of a recent, pioneering origin, such as the United States and Australia, civilisation now rests indeed with the "common man", and the surviving aristocratic element has become a cultural fossil. But the situation is not the same in countries with a strong continuous tradition, such as England, where fairly sharp class-distinctions survive in vocabulary, accent, tastes. That unique social amalgam of the lower fringes of the aristocracy and the top fringes of the mercantile bourgeoisie, known as the British upper middle class, has until recently provided the bulk of the nation's leaders in politics, literature and the arts; even the *avant-garde* of Marxist writers in the 'thirties mostly had double-barrelled names. Accordingly, the "interfering" scale of values is indeed based on a great cultural heritage. The obsessive preoccupation of the British intelligentsia with the aristocracy is perhaps partly excusable on these lines. But when all allowances are made, snobbery remains a grotesque affliction of English society, motivated by the naïve desire to feel part of, or at least rub shoulders with, a social élite, however much in decline that élite may be. The Crillon complex appears on this level as the fear of not being a full-fledged contemporary on the social scene where the Battles of Arques are fought at first nights and cocktail parties. "Pends-toi, brave Evelyn: nous avons diné à Blenheim et tu n'y étais pas."

8

So far I have not mentioned the most obvious and widespread motivation of social snobbery: the bolstering of the insecure ego by being accepted into the company of the high and mighty—whether these are represented by the titled, or moneyed, or artistic élite. But this kind of explanation of snobbery begs the question. The compensation of inferiority complexes is one of the basic psychological mechanisms; it does not explain why the snob seeks for compensation in his specific way. In his amusing essay on "Snobs",* Russell Lynes says: "The snob is almost by definition insecure in his social (in the larger sense) relationships, and resorts to snobbishness as a means of massaging his ego. Since scarcely anyone is so secure that his ego does not sometimes need a certain amount of external manipulation, there is scarcely anyone who isn't a snob of some sort." True as far as it goes; but there are as many ways of massaging one's ego as there are human activities. From Demosthenes, who compensated his inborn stammering by forcing himself to talk with his mouth full of pebbles until he became the foremost orator of Greece, to Napoleon, who made up for his short stature and lowly birth by conquering Europe, a feeling of inadequacy has always been a powerful motor of ambition. The real question is why the same compensatory drive is satisfied in one case by creative achievement, in another by grotesque and sterile attitudes. Most people are in need of "a certain amount of massaging of their egos"; but the snob needs, for his massage, an oil extracted from the olive groves overlooking the Blue Grotto of Capri.

Guided by an inappropriate standard of values, the snob's pursuits are sterile, and his satisfactions of a vicarious nature. He does not aim at power; he merely wants to rub shoulders with those

* New York, 1950.

who yield power, and bask in their reflected glory. A person with a genuine power drive would rather be top of a group of his equals than bottom of a superior group. The snob's ambition is the reverse: he would rather be the lowest-ranking and just tolerated hanger-on of the envied set or club, than a full-fledged member of the one to which by nature he belongs. He would rather stay in a stuffy cubbyhole in a luxury hotel than have a room with a bath and a view in the next-cheaper category; he does not seek the bodily comfort which makes luxury desirable, but the vicarious comfort of "staying at the Ritz". His social pleasures are equally perverted. He does not seek love, friendship, conviviality, but the cold, vicarious glow of being permitted to share the company of the select. The art snob's pleasures are not derived from the picture, but from the catalogue; the intellectual snob is not impressed by Kirkegard, he is impressed by himself reading Kirkegard. This perversion of values may even affect his biological instincts—his taste and smell preferences, his sexual inclinations. His procreative glands are stimulated not by Boccaccio, but by Debrett; and a hundred years ago, when oysters and stout were the diet of the poor, the snob's taste-buds functioned in a different manner.

To sum up: the snob's satisfactions do not derive from the object of his preoccupation, but from some secondary consideration associated with it; they are pseudo-satisfactions. His drives are imitative, his labours barren, his pleasures vicarious, his triumphs self-delusions. The perfect symbol of it all is the show-off TV aerial on the roof of suburban houses—minus the television set.

9

There's no doubt about it, the debutante of the nineteen-fifties has a harder life than most people imagine. Although (as a debutante was recently heard to remark) "Culture's the top thing really, and let's face it, that's a tiny bit of a bore", it isn't possible to devote the whole day to that.

HOUSEWIFE, April, 1954

To catalogue the various forms of snobbery would be a monumentally boring enterprise; I would like to mention, however, a few of the less obvious variants.

Take, for instance, the disrepute attached to the word "cleverness" in the idiom of the British upper classes, and the pride and delight its female members take in statements like: "I am hopeless about spelling", "about sums", "about geography and all that." Once upon a time, the *literati* were ill-paid scribes, and earlier on slaves, while the upper classes went about their seignorial pursuits. The contempt in which knowledge, "cleverness", "braininess", is still held in the more fossilised upper strata of society is a distant, yet direct, echo of those bygone days.

A more subtle distortion of our intellectual values is caused by the emphasis in public schools on the humanities and the corresponding neglect of the sciences; the roots of this tradition are equally easy to trace in the past. Its paradoxical result is that people feel humiliated if they have to admit that they have not heard the name of some third-rate poet or painter, but confess with pride their total ignorance of the laws which govern the heredity of their children or the working of the electric light. In relation to his mechanised environment, modern man is thus reduced to the intellectual level of the savage. He starts his car and does not know why it runs, switches on the gas and does not know why it burns, swallows a pill and does not know why it makes him sleep; but he talks glibly about existentialism, abstracts and *collage*.

In the social hierarchy, this state of affairs is reflected by the fact that the professions related to the humanities, the arts and letters rank higher than those connected with engineering and the applied sciences. The Central-European *Herr Ingenieur* is a gentleman and the French *politechniciens* are a social élite; an engineer in England hovers between the working and the middle class. One wonders to what extent the steady loss of ground by British industry to German and American competition is caused by this type of snobbery influencing vocational choice.

This perversion has its reverse side. The age of science has brought with it a growing emphasis on the quantitative, measurable aspects of all phenomena. By various methods of physical measurement, we have learnt to reduce quality to quantity; thus, for instance, we are able to reduce colour and sound to vibrational frequencies which can be expressed by simple figures. Similarly, we can express the qualities of objects, energies and movements by quantitative equations. This process has led to the dangerous mental habit not merely of *explaining* quality by quantity but of *replacing* the concept of quality by that of measurable quantity. In American parlance, a man is "worth" his bank account; the value of a painter is "quoted", and has its ups and downs like a share on the stock exchange; the value of a book is expressed by its rating on the best-seller list; the radio performances of a Bach cantata and of a sobbing crooner are compared on the same scale of audience-rating. This application of quantitative yardsticks to the measurement of quality is one of the most frightening perversions of values; yet essentially it is merely another variant at the mental confusion which makes the snob assess the æsthetic value of a picture by its age and provenance.

Another type of snobbery, produced by contempt for

cleverness, is the deliberate cultivation of personal mannerisms, the building up of an "anecdotical personality". In a society where it is considered bad conversational form to discuss anything in earnest, and good form to avert this danger by giving the subject an anecdotic twist, mannerisms are apt to grow like weeds, stifling intellectual exchange; and an eccentric, or at least slightly dotty façade, becomes the safest means of making an impression. Simplicity and directness are of no avail; the snob's ambition is not to have, but to be, "a character". Even great intellects are affected by the virus: Shaw's clowning, the donnishness of English dons, the studied stammer of the highbrow, the premium set on eccentricity, are symptoms of the prevalence of manner over mind.

An equally obvious phenomenon is inverted snobbery. A simple reversal of the conventional scale of values produces the athletes of modesty, the exhibitionists of self-effacement, the dandyism of black fingernails, the coquetry of ignorance. If we contrast the hyper-sensitive and hyper-articulate heroes of Proust with the dumb and inarticulate heroes of Hemingway, we have defined the range of literary snobbery on a reversible scale.

Lastly, I must mention the melancholy figure of the "knowing snob" who, unlike the naïve or genuine snob, knows that snobbery is a bad thing and yet admits with resigned insight that he cannot live without this delightful poison, or indispensable crutch, whichever the case may be. The purest examples of the knowing, self-despising, yet incurable category of snobs, are to be found among the English writers and artists of our time.

10

Is the poison really so delightful? I mentioned in a previous book that I have always wanted to write a sequel to La Fontaine's fable of *The Fox and the Grapes*. The poor fox, mocked by his friends, conscious of his defeat, develops an inferiority complex for which, he knows, there is only one cure. Night after night, while the other members of the pack are having a good time stealing nice, fat hens, he is secretly engaged in taking climbing lessons. After several weeks of dogged effort, he finally does succeed in getting at the grapes—only to find that a terrible disappointment has been waiting for him. The coveted grapes really *are* sour, as he had pretended from the beginning. But who will believe him? He himself can hardly believe that the beautiful, succulent-looking grapes are hard and acid as gall. The grapes become an obsession with him. He has to go on climbing after them, panting and sweating, and to go on eating the beastly fruit for the sole purpose of proving to himself that he is man enough, or fox enough, to reach them. He gets more and more skinny on this diet and, after a nervous breakdown, dies of gastric ulcers.

The parable is meant to illustrate the tragedy of snobs and careerists of the more intelligent kind. The sophisticated snob knows quite well that the select club or set into which he has gained admittance, after such strenuous efforts, is stale and uninspiring; yet he feels compelled to live off that arid vineyard to prove to himself that it is within his reach. The same is true of obsessional success-hunters in every field—film stars and business executives, career-girls and social hostesses. After the first successful climb they find out that the coveted fruit is not at all what they imagined it to be. Yet they live under the compulsion to go on sweating and straining and munching the bitter fruit to the bitter end.

Wherever we turn, the contemporary scene is populated by skinny foxes feasting on sour grapes. Only the most common and low-brow foxes take an interest in rabbits and hens. The result is a collective indigestion, a social neurosis on a vast and unprecedented scale which reflects the general distortion of values in all fields of modern civilisation.

Thus the all-pervading phenomenon of snobbery turns out to be a reflection of the spiritual crisis and of the moral and intellectual chaos which accompanies it. In the absence of any firm standards of value, it is inevitable that the wrong scale should be applied to the wrong object. Modern man gropes his way through this confusing world, armed with a compass which always points in the wrong direction, and a measuring rod which, a reversal of the magic wand, turns everything it touches to dust; engaged in shadow pursuits which provide him with shadow satisfactions in the metaphysical darkness.

The Future of the Novel *

1

NOVELS DATE more than drama and poetry. The reason for this is the novel's pseudo-objectivity. The characters on the stage speak for themselves; the poet, whose method is direct and subjective, speaks for himself; but in the novel the author speaks for his characters, and pretends to give an objective account of their thoughts, feelings and actions. This alleged objectivity is, of course, pure swindle. For the narrative reflects not only the author's personal philosophy, idiosyncrasies and style (that in itself would be all right) but also smuggles in, still under the label of objectivity, the whole baggage of the prejudices and conventions of his time. As the narrator, *ex hypothesi*, is omniscient, ubiquitous and non-existent as a person, it is the period itself which speaks through him. The novel's period-character is implicit and mainly unconscious, therefore all the more revealing.

2

Elizabeth Bowen said somewhere that the object of the novel is the non-poetic statement of a poetic truth. As a recent convert to semantics, I began to doubt whether I knew what a poetic

* First published as a contribution to a symposium in *New Writing and Daylight*, September, 1946.

truth is, though I always thought I did. I imagined Professor Ogden taking the class:

"In current usage we call a scientific truth a statement of the type that the attraction of a heavy body decreases in inverse ratio to the square of the distance. Now, Bowen, will you give us an example of what you call a statement of 'poetic' truth?"—"The wine-dark sea, I suppose."—"Is that a *statement*, Bowen? And how, by expressing it in non-poetical form, is it supposed to become a novel?"

Still, I side with Miss Bowen, but her formula needs elucidation. As a next step I suggest this phrase of Gerhardt Hauptman's: "Poetry is the distant echo of the primitive word behind the veil of words." It seems to me that the action of the novel is always the distant echo of some primitive action behind the veil of the period's costumes and conventions. The word "primitive" is used here in the sense of the archaic and perennial, the Jungian archetype. Archetypes are ever-repeated typical experiences rooted in the human condition; inherited patterns of instinct-conflicts; the psychic residue of the "suffering and delight that has happened countless times in our ancestral history, and on the average follows ever the same course".

The great significant works in the history of fiction are variations of such archetypal situations and conflicts, which first occur in mythology, and are re-stated in the specific language of the period. Prometheus, Job, Sisyphus, Samson, Oedipus, Tantalus, Narcissus, etc., are the eternal "stories" of the inadequacy of the human condition. Their listing would be a gratifying task for a research thesis. Here is one example: the type of story based on the archetypal figure of the "idiot", the inspired fool. Its heroes are ever-new incarnations of the ideas of charity and innocence. They appear to their environment as naïve, foolish, even mentally deficient—not because they lack intelligence, but because their system of values differs from the conventional values of their surroundings. Their simplicity moves on a higher plane than the craftiness of their time; so that their clever contemporaries, when they look down at them, have to lift their faces upward. Equally typical is the narrator's attitude to his hero: a tender ridicule, a sigh of regret for his own lack of courage to take the hero quite seriously, for alas, one has to keep one's feet on the earth. Examples of this chain are: the *Perceval legend*; the *Lay of the Great Fool*; the Welsh and Germanic variations of it; *Don Quixote*; *Eulenspiegel*; numerous variations of the *enfant terrible* and the "gentle-savage-goes-to-town" themes; Masereel's *The Sun*; Shaw's *Black Girl in Search of God*; Dostoevski's *The Idiot*; Thornton Wilder's *Heaven is my Destination*; Camus' *L'Étranger* (with a new twist); and so on. Other frequently recurring archetypes are: conflict between two loyalties (Penelope *v.* Trojan war, Katinka and the Five Year Plan); between instinct and convention (Bovary, Karenina); sensitive hero and callous world (all public-school novels and most autobiographies); shock and conversion (a Russian speciality but also a favourite motif with E. M. Forster); the conquest of fear (from Hercules to Hemingway) and of the flesh (from Buddha to Huxley). There are perhaps a dozen or so more—but not much more. The themes of fiction are limited; only their variations are inexhaustible.

Novels which are not fed from archetypal sources are shallow or phoney. They are like a house with elaborate plumbing, bathrooms, cold- and hot-water taps, which the builder forgot to connect with the main.

3

We may thus distinguish in the novel a constant and a variable factor. The constants are the archetypes, the predicaments inherent in the human condition. The variable factor is the cultural pattern of the period, and its conscious and unconscious techniques of projection.

As far as the first factor is concerned, we need not worry about the novel's future. Novelists will not run out of themes as long as mankind has not reached a state of nirvanic perfection and diffused its emotions in social entropy. Moreover, their themes will always remain new, for archetypes enjoy eternal youth like their early incarnations, the Olympians.

As to the variable factor, my prediction is that the fiction of the period between the second and the third world war will be dominated by a trend towards three Rs: Realism, Relevance, Rhythm.

By *Realism*, I mean neither the naturalism of Zola, nor the philosophy of Babbitt, the diplomacy of M. Vishinski, or the portraits in the Royal Academy. Realism in fiction is the striving to approach the reality of the human condition with as open a mind and as much disregard for convention, prejudice and habit as one's capacities permit. It means discarding traditions which mask vital bands in the human spectrum, and taking in new extensions of the visible range offered by psychology, the social sciences, the evolution of language. The opposite of realism is smugness, and the ambition to be recommended by the Book Society. Realism requires courage and integrity. But alas, these manly virtues are not enough; the less spectacular and more difficult task of realism is to assimilate the new extensions of the spectrum—and to assimilate them so completely that no residue of learnedness, no label of the scientific department-store should remain.

Some critics deny the necessity for the artist to take in new extensions of the spectrum. They wallow in statements like "Stendhal knew all that long before Freud" and "Tolstoi wouldn't have gained much by reading Marx." One might as well say that it makes no difference to the writer whether he knows that the earth is a small planet or believes that it is a disc supported by Atlas, and the centre of the world.

The approach to realism in the history of fiction is gradual. In the average Victorian novel, the whole range of sex was represented by a gap in the spectrum. To-day, a number of its aspects are admitted; but it would be naïve to believe that these suffice to cover even the most recurrent unmentionable thoughts and emotions of real people. A writer may take his courage into both hands and allude to some of them; yet he won't be able to do it with grace and ease. The passage will hit the reader in the eye, and the author will feel that he is handling a hammer. The novel will not be able to digest the full implications of Freud for perhaps another half-century. Art is not yet ripe to represent the most fundamental act of reality, procreation; even a Hemingway fails when he tries it.

4

Relevance is a quality in fiction which connects it with the dynamic currents, the essential pattern, of the period. In our period, these currents have become tidal waves which spare no private island. It is no longer a question whether ivory towers are desirable; the point is that they have become physically impossible. One could easily ignore the Boer War and the Dreyfus affair; one cannot escape the implications of the atom bomb. As public concerns invade an ever-increasing sector of the space inside the individual's skull, his private interests become increasingly saturated with relevance. The fiction of the next few decades will be situated in a strong magnetic field which will impose its pattern on the raw material as on a heap of iron filings. This is true even of the deliberately escapist type of fiction. George Orwell has recently analysed the development of the crime story from *Raffles* to *Miss Blandish*; similar conclusions could be reached by comparing the progress of "Romance" from the Victorian to the contemporary magazine story; or the evolution of humour from *Punch* to the *New Yorker*.

Finally, *Rhythm*. The rhythm of a narrative is a measure of its artistic economy; and economy is not brevity, but implicitness. Implicitness is a technique which forces the reader to work out for himself what is implied. Language itself is never completely explicit; words are mere stepping-stones for thoughts.[*] When listening to speech, we have continuously to establish connections between the words; otherwise, as when our attention flags, they become a mere medley of sounds. Economy in art thus has its roots in the basic mechanism of communicating thought-contents by acoustic or optic signs, and is a purposeful development of it. The reader has to fill in the gaps by drawing his own conclusions and projecting his own emotions; economy compels the consumer to re-live the producer's creative effort. The artist rules his subjects by turning them into accomplices.

Civilisation accelerates the rhythm of art, not because cars run faster but because thoughts run faster. Newspapers, radio, mass-produced books, have beaten and smoothed our associative pathways, and established a network of fast-running association trains where the Victorian reader's imagination ambled in a mailcoach. This does not mean that the rhythm of the narrative must necessarily become hectic and jumpy like Dos Passos' camera eye, or syncopated like a Hemingway dialogue. Nor should the narrator run after the thought-train like Joyce. His function is rather that of the pointsman's at the switchbox.

5

If one analyses any true novel, that is to say, a novel in which the conflict arises from the interplay of character and environment

* "They" are more than that... (!)

and bears the stamp of inescapability, one always arrives at a mythological core. The *leitmotifs* are timeless, but the orchestration is period-bound. The modes and moods of a given period form a sociological pattern; the individual threads in it must be seen both in the light of their archetypal origin and of their social context. If one of these conditions is missing, the novel will be a failure. But if both are fulfilled, something strange will happen. As with every living organism, you will get more out of it than you put in. It will not only describe, it will point. The novelist should never aim at more than stating; but if his echo does not bear a message, he has failed. Every philosophical, scientific, or artistic statement which is true, not only describes the world but changes it.

The antithesis to art is propaganda, where the emphasis is not on stating, but on changing. Hence the paradoxical result that, in order to change the world, the artist must forget his desire to do so. Since most writers have strong feelings about politics or other matters, the above sounds like an injunction to walk the tight-rope—which it is; but it is attenuated by the artist's inborn or acquired skill at walking the tight-rope in his sleep.

6

If we accept the three Rs as a tentative scale of measurement for the dominant trends in fiction, we are forced to conclude that the English novel is falling behind the French and American. The French are ahead of us in realism and relevance; the Americans, in realism and rhythm. The reasons cannot be analysed here. One of them is that to be a novelist has come to be regarded too much as a respectable profession in England—almost like being a solicitor or public trustee.

A Rebel's Progress

TO GEORGE ORWELL'S DEATH★

To MEET one's favourite author in the flesh is mostly a disillusioning experience. George Orwell was one of the few writers who looked and behaved exactly as the reader of his books expected him to look and behave. This exceptional concordance between the man and his work was a measure of the exceptional unity and integrity of his character.

An English critic recently called him the most honest writer alive; his uncompromising intellectual honesty was such that it made him appear almost inhuman at times. There was an emanation of austere harshness around him which diminished only in proportion to distance, as it were: he was merciless towards himself, severe upon his friends, unresponsive to admirers, but full of understanding sympathy for those on the remote periphery, the "crowds in the big towns with their knobby faces, their bad teeth and gentle manners; the queues outside the Labour Exchanges, the old maids biking to Holy Communion through the mists of the autumn mornings . . ."

Thus, the greater the distance from intimacy and the wider the radius of the circle, the more warming became the radiations of this lonely man's great power of love. But he was incapable of self-love or self-pity. His ruthlessness towards himself was the key

★ First published in *The Observer*, 29th January, 1950.

to his personality; it determined his attitude towards the enemy within, the disease which had raged in his chest since his adolescence.

His life was one consistent series of rebellions both against the condition of society in general and his own particular predicament; against humanity's drift towards 1984 and his own drift towards the final breakdown. Intermittent hæmorrhages marked like milestones the rebel's progress as a sergeant in the Burma police, a dishwasher in Paris, a tramp in England, a soldier in Spain. Each should have acted as a warning, and each served as a challenge, answered by works of increasing weight and stature.

The last warning came three years ago. It became obvious that his life-span could only be prolonged by a sheltered existence under constant medical care. He chose to live instead on a lonely island in the Hebrides, with his adopted baby son, without even a charwoman to look after him.

Under these conditions he wrote his savage vision of 1984. Shortly after the book was completed he became bedridden, and never recovered. Yet had he followed the advice of doctors and friends, and lived in the self-indulgent atmosphere of a Swiss sanatorium, his masterpiece could not have been written—nor any of his former books. The greatness and tragedy of Orwell was his total rejection of compromise.

The urge of genius and the promptings of common sense can rarely be reconciled; Orwell's life was a victory of the former over the latter. For now that he is dead, the time has come to recognise that he was the only writer of genius among the *littérateurs* of social revolt between the two wars. Cyril Connolly's remark, referring to their common prep-school days: "I was a stage rebel, Orwell a true one," is valid for his whole generation.

When he went to fight in Spain he did not join the sham-fraternity of the International Brigades, but the most wretched of the Spanish Milicia units, the heretics of the P.O.U.M. He was the only one whom his grim integrity kept immune against the spurious *mystique* of the "Movement," who never became a fellow-traveller and never believed in Moses the Raven's Sugar-candy Mountain—either in heaven or on earth. Consequently, his seven books of that period, from *Down and Out* to *Coming up for Air* all remain fresh and bursting with life, and will remain so for decades to come, whereas most of the books produced by the "emotionally shallow Leftism" of that time, which Orwell so despised, are dead and dated to-day.

A similar comparison could be drawn for the period of the war. Among all the pamphlets, tracts and exhortations which the war produced, hardly anything bears re-reading to-day—except, perhaps, E. M. Forster's *What I Believe*, a few passages from Churchill's speeches, and, above all, Orwell's *The Lion and the Unicorn*. Its opening section, "England Your England," is one of the most moving and yet incisive portraits of the English character, and a minor classic in itself.

Animal Farm and *1984* are Orwell's last works. No parable was written since *Gulliver's Travels* equal in profundity and mordant satire to *Animal Farm*, no fantasy since Kafka's *In the Penal Settlement* equal in logical horror to *1984*. I believe that future historians of literature will regard Orwell as a kind of missing link between Kafka and Swift. For, to quote Connolly again, it may well be true that "it is closing time in the gardens of the West, and from now on an artist will be judged only by the resonance of his solitude or the quality of his despair".

The resonance of Orwell's solitude and the quality of his despair can only be compared to Kafka's—but with this difference: that Orwell's despair had a concrete, organised structure, as it were, and was projected from the individual to the social plane. And if "four legs good, two legs bad," is pure Swift, there is again this difference: that Orwell never completely lost faith in the knobby-faced yahoos with their bad teeth. Had he proposed an epitaph for himself, my guess is that he would have chosen these lines from Old Major's revolutionary anthem, to be sung to a "stirring tune, something between 'Clementine' and 'La Cucuracha'":

> *Rings shall vanish from our noses,*
> *And the harness from our back . . .*
>
> *For that day we all must labour,*
> *Though we die before it break;*
> *Cows and horses, geese and turkeys,*
> *All must toil for freedom's sake.*

Somehow Orwell really believed in this. It was this quaint belief which guided the rebel's progress, and made him so very lovable though he did not know it.

Judah at the Crossroads

AN EXHORTATION *

THE MARTYRDOM of the Jews runs like a jagged scar across the face of human history. The resurrection of the State of Israel offers, for the first time in two thousand years, the possibility of solving the Jewish problem. Up to now the Jews' fate lay in the hands of the Gentiles. At present, it lies entirely in their own hands. The wandering Jew has arrived at a crossroads, and the consequences of his present choice will make themselves felt for centuries to come.

The total Jewish population of the world is at present estimated at eleven and a half millions. On the European Continent the National Socialist régime nearly succeeded in eliminating the previously strong and culturally significant Jewish community. Out of a pre-war population of six million Jews (excluding Russia), only one million, that is, approximately fifteen in a hundred, survived in 1946. In Berlin and Vienna, in Warsaw and Prague, where Jews had played an important and at times dominant part in cultural life, their influence has completely disappeared. The first question which the Jews now have to decide is whether it is desirable that the void should again be filled. Should they flock back into these areas, which have become the

* This essay follows to their conclusion certain thoughts and suggestions tentatively expressed in *Promise and Fulfilment* (1950); I have used passages from that book, and from my earlier *Thieves in the Night* without quotation marks.

cemeteries of their kin, should they try to regain their former positions in finance, industry, literature, journalism, the arts and sciences, while retaining their separate identity as Jews, and thereby resuscitate the "Jewish problem" in Europe? The question must be answered in the light of past experience, and of the new reality created by the State of Israel.

In the United States, where the major part of contemporary Jewry lives, the problem arises in a different form: should the American Jews aim at maintaining their separateness as a religious and social community, or at gradually eliminating it?

In the third geographical area where Jews live in large numbers, the territories East of the Iron Curtain, the question is less acute. The pressure of the anti-religious totalitarian State (in spite of temporary oscillations of the line) is gradually eliminating the institutions and traditions on which Jewish separateness depended: the synagogue, the Yiddish language, Jewish residential districts and even Jewish surnames. If these régimes survive the next two or three generations, there will be little or no trace left of a separate Jewish community in the religious and ethnical sense.

But in Western Europe and America, and in every other part of the world where Jews exist in sizeable numbers, the dilemma arising out of the creation of the Jewish State is grave and acute, though the majority of them do not as yet realize its full implications, and the fateful choice it imposes on them. To put it bluntly, it is the choice between either becoming a citizen of Israel, or ceasing to be a Jew in the national, religious, or any other meaning of the word. The choice is imposed by historic circumstance and by the essential content of the Jewish tradition itself.

2

The ultimate distinguishing mark of the Jew (I shall come back to this point later) is not his race, language or culture, but his religion. It officially defines him as a Jew from the moment of his birth, it is the original source of his social and cultural peculiarities, and of his self-awareness as a Jew.

Unlike any other religion, however, the Mosaic religion is inseparably tied to the idea of a separate nation. One can be a Catholic or a Protestant, a Moslem or a Buddhist, regardless of nationality or race. But the Jewish faith implies membership of a historic nation with a land of its own, from which it has been temporarily exiled. Christianity and Islam only demand from their followers that they accept certain doctrines and ethical rules which transcend frontiers and nations; the Jewish believer professes to belong to a chosen race, the seed of Abraham, Isaac and Jacob, with whom God made a covenant including the promise of preferential treatment and of a geographical home. "Blessed be the Lord, our God, who led our fathers out of the bondage in Egypt"—the person who recites that prayer claims a racial ancestry (whether biologically he is right or not) which automatically sets him apart from the racial and historic past of the people in whose midst he lives. A comparison between Christian and Jewish festivals reveals the significant fact that the former are sacred, the latter all secular in character. Christians celebrate mystical or mythological events: the birth and resurrection of the Son of God, the assumption of the Virgin; Jews commemorate landmarks in national history: the Maccabean revolt, the exodus from Egypt, the death of the oppressor Haman, the destruction of the Temple. The Old Testament is first and foremost the history book of a nation; every prayer and ritual observance strengthens the Jew's consciousness of his national identity. The claim that Judaism is "a religion like other religions, a private affair which has nothing to do with politics or race" is either hypocritical or self-contradictory. *The Jewish faith is nationally and racially self-segregating.* It automatically creates its own cultural and ethnic ghettoes.

Judah at the Crossroads

At the end of the Passover meal, Jews all over the world during the last two thousand years have lifted their glasses and drunk a sacred toast to "next year in Jerusalem". Thus the Jewish religion postulates not only a national past, but also a national future. The Proclamation of Independence of the Jewish State, issued on 14th May, 1948, declares: "Exiled from the land of Israel, the Jewish people remained faithful to it in all the countries of their dispersion, never ceasing to pray and hope for their return and the restoration of national freedom." Jews refer to the last two millennia of their history as the Diaspora, or Age of Dispersion, and to all countries outside Palestine as "the Galuth" or "the Lands of Exile". His faith thus compels the Jewish believer to regard himself as a person with a national past and future different from that of the Gentiles among whom he lives. The "Englishman of Jewish faith" becomes a contradiction in terms. As a member of the chosen race, temporarily exiled from his promised land, he is not an English Jew, but a Jew living in England. This refers not only to conscious Zionists, but to all members of the Jewish community who, whatever their attitude to Zionism and Palestine, are bound to regard themselves, by the articles of their faith, as members of a separate race with a separate national past and future. The fact that they are unaware, or only half aware of the secular implications of their creed, and that the majority indignantly reject "racial discrimination" if it comes from the other camp, makes the Jewish tradition only more paradoxical and self-contradictory.

Racial discrimination does indeed work both ways. The tendency, even among liberal and enlightened Jews, to seek each other's company, to keep themselves to themselves in marriage and social life, is only partly due to the pressure of hostile surroundings. An equally important bond is tradition with an ethnic and national tinge. Catholic minorities in Protestant countries sometimes display an apparently similar tendency towards solidarity. But the analogy is misleading, for this solidarity—or cliquishness—is confined to Catholics with strong feelings about their faith, or at least about the position of their Church in the world. Jewish cliquishness, on the other hand, extends to members of the community who hold no religious convictions, are indifferent to Zionism, regard themselves as hundred per cent. Americans or Englishmen, and yet cling together, tied by shared habits and tastes, by an inert tradition voided of all spiritual content which, to quote Arnold Toynbee, is merely "the fossilized remnant of a once independent culture".

A further symptom of the discriminatory character of Judaism is the Jewish attitude to the Gentile. That twenty centuries of persecution must leave their marks of suspicion and defensive hostility, we take for granted; the point is too obvious to need elaboration. But the Jewish attitude to the Stranger in Israel carries an original element of rejection which is historically older than the ghettoes, which dates back to the tribal exclusiveness of the Mosaic religion. The Hebrew word "Goy" which designates the non-Jew does not merely mean "pagan" or "unbeliever"; it does not refer to a soul capable of salvation or a body capable of being accepted into the community after acquiring the true faith. The "Goy" corresponds rather to the Greeks' "Barbarian", to our "natives" and "aborigines". It refers not to a religious, but to a racial and ethnic distinction. In spite of occasional, and somewhat half-hearted, injunctions to be kind to the Stranger in Israel, the Goy is treated in the Old Testament with a mixture of hostility, contempt and pity, as not really quite up to human standards. In the centuries that have passed since, the concept of the Goy has lost some of its tribal emotionalism, but it has never entirely lost its derogatory echo. In the ghettoes of Poland, the young men sang mocking songs about the drunken Goy, which were no nobler in spirit than the anti-semitic jingles about Kikes and Yids. A persecuted minority certainly has good excuses for repaying hostility and contempt in the same coin, but the point I wish to make is that we are faced with a vicious circle: that a religion with the secular claim of racial exclusiveness must needs create secular repercussions. The Jew's religion sets him apart and invites his being set apart. The archaic, tribal element in it engenders anti-semitism on the same archaic level. No amount of enlightenment and tolerance, of indignant protests and pious exhortations, can break this vicious circle.

"Anti-semitism is a disease that spreads apparently according to its own laws: I believe the only fundamental cause of anti-semitism—it may seem tautological—is that the Jew exists. We seem to carry anti-semitism in our knapsacks wherever we go." This was said by the late Professor Chaim Weizmann, first President of the resurrected Jewish State, in summing up the calvary of twenty long centuries. To expect that it will come to a spontaneous end in the twenty-first is to go against historic and psychological evidence, against the law of cause and effect. It can only be brought to an end by Jewry itself. But neither President Weizmann nor any of the Jewish leaders of our time had the courage to face this fact and to speak out openly.

To come back to my starting-point: the general distinguishing mark of the Jew, that which makes him a Jew on his documents and in the eyes of his fellow-citizens, is his religion; and the Jewish religion, unlike any other, is racially discriminatory, nationally segregative, socially tension-creating. Once this basic fact—supported by the evidence of the five volumes of the Old Testament, the hundreds of volumes of sacred commentaries, and the common book of Jewish prayers—is firmly and uncontroversially established in our minds, and the unconscious resistances against accepting it as a fact are overcome, then the first step towards solving the problem has been made.

The emphasis here is on the "unconscious resistances" which, as we shall see later, are immensely and understandably strong among all who, by faith or tradition, claim to be Jews. For the moment, however, I shall leave the psychological aspect aside, and proceed with my argument.

3

Let us distinguish between three categories of Jews: (a) the minority of orthodox believers, (b) the larger group of the adherents of a liberalised and diluted version of the Mosaic religion, (c) the largest group of agnostics, who, for complex reasons of tradition or pride, persist in calling themselves and their children "Jews".

The orthodox believers outside the State of Israel are a small and dwindling minority. The stronghold of orthodox Jewry was Eastern Europe—Poland, Latvia, Lithuania, Ruthenia— where the Nazi fury reached its peak and wiped them almost completely off the face of the earth. The scattered survivors, and the small orthodox groups in the United States, are composed mostly of elderly people. Orthodoxy is dying out in the Western world, while the bulk of the strictly tradition-bound communities in North Africa, the Yemen, Syria and Iraq are emigrating to Israel.

Thus, as a social group the remnants of orthodox Jewry no longer carry much weight. But their position is symbolical of the dilemma that confronts Judaism at large. Since the burning down of the Temple they have never ceased to pray for the restoration of the Jewish State, for "next year in Jerusalem". On 14th May, 1948, their prayer was suddenly fulfilled. Now the logical consequence of the fulfilment of a prayer is that one ceases to repeat it. But if prayers of this kind are no longer repeated, if the mystic yearning for the return to Palestine is eliminated from the Jewish faith, then the very foundations and essence of that faith will have gone. No obstacle prevents any longer any orthodox Jew from obtaining a visa at the Israeli Consulate, and booking a passage on the Israeli Line. The alternative before him is either to be "next year in Jerusalem", or to cease repeating a vow which has become mere lip-service.

In fact the major part of Judaism's prayers, rites, and symbols have become meaningless since the restoration of the Jewish State. To persist in them in the future would be as anachronistic and absurd as if Christians persisted in secretly gathering in catacombs, or Lutherans continued reading their Bible in secret. The Proclamation of Independence of the State of Israel affirms that it "will be open to Jews from all the countries of their dispersion". On the eve of Sabbath the ramhorn sounds again in the streets of Jerusalem to call the faithful to worship. The Lord of Israel has kept the Covenant and returned Canaan to Abraham's seed. The Orthodox Jew can no longer refer to himself with the ritual phrase as living "in exile"—unless he means a self-imposed exile, based on economic considerations which have nothing to do with his religion. If he refuses to obey the commandment to return to the land of his fathers, he places himself outside the Covenant and excommunicates himself according to his own terms of reference—though of course he will never admit it.

The orthodox position typifies in an extreme form the dilemma that is inherent in any liberalised and reformed version of Judaism. I have dwelt at length on the essentially racial and national character of the Jewish religion. Any attempted reform, however enlightened, which aims at eliminating this specific content of Judaism would eliminate its very essence. Take away the "Chosen Race" idea, the genealogical claim of descent from one of the twelve tribes, the focal interest in Palestine as the *locus* of a glorious past, and the memories of national history perpetuated in the religious festivals; take away the promise of a return to the Holy Land—and all that remained would be a set of archaic dietary prescriptions and tribal laws. It would not be the reform of a religion but its complete emaciation, and a turning back of the clock to the Bronze Age.

Let us now consider the position of that vast majority of contemporary Jewry who display an enlightened or sceptical attitude towards the faith of their ancestors, yet for a number of complex motives persist in confirming their children in that faith and impose on them the "separateness" that it entails. Paradoxically, it is this type of "nondescript" Jew, unable to define his Jewishness in either racial or religious terms, who perpetuates the "Jewish question".

In dealing with this central problem, I shall repeatedly quote from Isaiah Berlin's series of articles, "Jewish Slavery and Emancipation"*, which has come to be regarded as a classic treatment of the subject. Berlin starts by agreeing that "there is no possible argument against those truly religious Jews to whom the preservation of Judaism as a faith is an absolute obligation to which everything, including life itself, must without hesitation be sacrificed", and later on endorses the view that for these full-blooded Jews, as it were, the only logical solution is emigration to Israel. He then turns to the "nondescript" category and says:

" . . . But it is not so clear that those who believe in the preservation and transmission of 'Jewish values' (which are usually something less than a complete religious faith, but rather an amalgam of attitudes, cultural outlook, racial memories and feelings, personal and social habits) are justified in assuming without question that this form of life is obviously worth saving, even at the unbelievable cost in blood and tears which has made the history of the Jews for two thousand years a dreadful martyrology. Once . . . unreasoning faith is diluted into loyalty to traditional forms of life, even though it be sanctified by history and the suffering and faith of heroes and

* *Jewish Chronicle*, June, 1950.

martyrs in every generation, alternative possibilities can no longer be dismissed out of hand."

The only alternative to the perpetuation of Jewish separateness for that nondescript majority who have outgrown Jewish nationalism and the Jewish religion, is to renounce both, and to allow themselves to be socially and culturally absorbed by their environment. All that I have said before leads up to this harsh but inescapable conclusion.

Yet the psychological resistances against it are enormous. The springs of this resistance are partly to be found in the general human tendency to avoid a painful choice. But equally important emotional factors are spiritual pride, civic courage, the apprehension of being accused of hypocrisy or cowardice, the scars of wounds inflicted in the past, the reluctance to abandon a mystic destiny, a specifically Jewish mission.

Let me concede at once that psychologically there is every excuse for Jews being emotional, illogical and touchy on the question of renunciation—even if they are unable to say what exactly they are reluctant to renounce. But let it be also clear that, while every man has a right to act irrationally and against his own interests, he has no right to act in this way where the future of his children is concerned. I would like to make it clear at this point that my whole line of argument, and the practical conclusions derived from it, are aimed not at the present, but at the next generation, at the decisions which men and women who were brought up in the Jewish community must take regarding not their own status, but the future of their children. Once this point is clearly established, a number of objections against the process of assimilation will be automatically removed.

I shall now consider some typical objections which were raised since, several years ago, I first proposed the solution advocated in these lines. They are well summarised in the questions put to me by an interviewer from the London *Jewish Chronicle* after the publication of my book *Promise and Fulfilment* in which I had tentatively broached the subject. The interviewer was Mr. Maurice Carr, and the interview, from which the following extracts are quoted, appeared in the official weekly paper of British Jewry under the headline "Arthur Koestler's Renunciation".* It opened with a long introductory remark by Mr. Carr:

"... *I was anxious to obtain* [*the author's comments*] *to the Epilogue in his book* Promise and Fulfilment *whose message may be summed up in this one brief passage:*

'*The existence of the Hebrew State . . . puts every Jew outside Israel before a dilemma which will become increasingly acute. It is the choice between becoming a citizen of the Hebrew nation and renouncing any conscious or implicit claim to separate nationhood.*'

. . . If that was what Arthur Koestler really meant, then it seemed to me, willy-nilly, he was placing himself in the evil company of the professional anti-Semites, who, with the logic of violence, bedaub the walls with the slogan: '*Jew go to Israel or into the crematorium!*' *. . . The ineffable quality of Jewishness, having weathered so many cataclysmic storms in the past, will no doubt resist Arthur Koestler's assault upon it.*"

(*Question*): When you say categorically that the Wandering Jew must decide either to become an Israeli or to renounce utterly his Jewishness, are you thinking in ultimate or immediate terms?

(*Answer*): I think that the choice must be made here and now, for the next generation's sake. The time has come for every Jew to ask himself: Do I really consider myself a member of a

* *Jewish Chronicle, 5th May, 1950.*

Chosen Race destined to return from exile to the Promised Land? In other words: Do I want to emigrate to Israel? And if not, what right have I to go on calling myself a Jew and thereby inflicting on my children the stigma of otherliness? Unless one shares the Nazis' racial theories, one has to admit that there is no such thing as a pure Jewish race. The primary distinguishing mark of the Jew is his religion. But this religion becomes meaningless if you go on praying for the Return to Zion even while you are firmly resolved to stay away. What then remains of your Jewishness? Not much more than the habit of regarding yourself, and being looked upon by others, as an outsider. But you thereby condemn your children to unwholesome environmental pressures which at best create handicaps of varying severity for their inner development and public career, and at worst lead to Belsen and Auschwitz.

(Q.): Is your haste in proclaiming the choice between Israel and total abandonment of Jewishness attributable to the fear of new Belsens and Auschwitzes?

(A.): Anti-Semitism is growing. Even the British, for all their traditional tolerance, have recently been affected, otherwise they wouldn't have swallowed Mr. Bevin's Palestine policy. But, to my mind, it is not so much the danger of pogroms as the fundamental evil of abnormal environmental pressures from which the Wandering Jew must save himself and the coming generations.

(Q.): Does it not occur to you that in seeking the will-o'-the-wisp of "normality" and security, runaway Jewry will be sacrificing the distinctive Jewish genius: and do you not consider, from the broadest humanist viewpoint, that such a loss of the Jewish heritage and of Jewish talents will more than outweigh any problematic gains?

(A.): It is undoubtedly true that the stimulus of environmental pressure has produced a greater proportion of intellectuals among Jews than among their host nations. This process of "over-compensation" is familiar both to the psychologist and the historian—see in particular Adler and Toynbee. We also know that most great men in literature, art, politics, religion, had an unhappy childhood, were lonely and misunderstood, and that their creative achievements were partly due to their reactions to these pressure-stimuli. But would you recommend parents to give their children deliberately an unhappy childhood in the hope of breeding an Einstein, a Freud, or a Heine? Of course, abolish all suffering in the world and you would abolish the chance of producing outstanding personalities. But, after all, out of 1,000 individuals subjected to unhealthy environmental pressure, 999 will develop thwarted characters and only one will perhaps become an outstanding personality. I reject as wholly indefensible the vague Jewish sentiment: "We must go on being persecuted in order to produce geniuses."

As for the Jewish cultural heritage, the Scriptures and Apocrypha have become the common property of mankind. The Talmud is to-day of interest only to a narrow specialised group. To impose a study of it, and of Biblical exegesis, on Jewish children in general is as utterly absurd and sterile as it would be to compel all Christian children to study medieval scholasticism. By way of secular culture you have mainly modern Yiddish literature: but the Yiddish language was killed with the people who spoke it in Eastern Europe, and I don't suppose you would defend its survival in America any more than of Ukrainian. The only legitimate, natural home for the preservation and future growth of a specifically Jewish culture is Israel.

(Q.): How do you reconcile your dictum "the means justify the end" with your advice to the Wandering Jew to run away from himself? After the first cowardly step of abdication, surely the renegade Jew will have to stoop to gross deceitfulness, resolutely lying to himself, to his neighbours, and to his children about his Jewish origin. Otherwise, if he chooses to be honest and disdains concealment, neither he nor his children will become thoroughgoing non-Jews. Rather will they merely become "ex-Jews". Will not then an ex-Jew be a new sort of freakish outsider, certainly spurned by the Jews, and in all probability still derided by the anti-Semites?

(*A.*): To-day every Jew has the possibility of going to Israel, so it is no longer an act of cowardice to choose the alternative of renouncing one's Jewishness. It has become a voluntary renunciation, which before the rebirth of Israel it was not. . . . To cling to an outworn status of "negative Jewishness" out of sheer stubbornness or from fear of being called a coward, is in itself an inverted form of cowardice for which helpless children will be made to suffer. As to the quality of honesty, that is the very thing I am advocating. It takes an equal measure of uncompromising honesty for one Jew to opt for "next year in Jerusalem" and for another Jew to decide on renunciation. He who abandons Jewishness should not conceal anything from his children; nor on the other hand need he bother the children prematurely. After all, it is a question of tact and delicacy, rather like the problem of education on sexual matters.

(Q.): Of all the Jews persecuted by Hitler, none suffered such terrible despair as those who had thought to cast off all traces of their own or their father's or their grandmother's Jewishness. In one form or another, might not a similarly cruel fate—far worse than that which can ever befall a real Jew—overtake the would-be ex-Jews?

(*A.*): Whatever one does in life, there is always the chance that something will go wrong. But I am certain that by and large the Gentile world will welcome wholehearted Jewish assimilation. Individual complications may arise, especially in the first and second generations, but thereafter—what with mixed marriages—the Jewish problem will gradually disappear to the benefit of all concerned.

(Q.): What religious education, if any, would you suggest for the children of ex-Jews?

(A.): First let me make it clear that when I advocate the renunciation of the Jewish faith by those who are unwilling to live according to its tenets (that is, to return to the Promised Land) I emphatically do *not* advocate their conversion to any other religion—unless of course they feel spiritually and sincerely attracted to it. This would be contemptible hypocrisy. But I do advocate with equal emphasis that the *children* of these "ex-Jews" who are not yet either spiritually or formally committed to the Jewish creed which their parents have abandoned, should be brought up like the other children of the environment in which they live. If the other children at their school go to church or chapel, let them go to church or chapel, and do not brand them as different. No new-born babe has a say in the question to which denomination it should belong, and the usual practice in the world to-day is that parents who have no specific religious convictions leave the religious formation of their children to the hazards of school and environment. I believe it is essential for a child to start his spiritual development with a belief in God, regardless whether this is a Jewish, Calvinist, or Wesleyan God, and to be left to make his decision in matters religious when he reaches maturity. To put it bluntly, I regard it as an outright crime for parents who neither believe in Jewish doctrine nor live up to its commandments, to impose the stigma of "otherliness" on a defenceless child who has not asked for it.

(Q.): Do you not feel that there is something abject, humiliating, in such a conformist surrender by the minority to the majority? Without any belief in, say, Catholicism, the ex-Jew is to send his children to a Jesuit school. He is to bury alive his own traditions and memories, and these memories, unfortunately, include bitter persecution at the hands of those whose ranks he is now joining uninvited. Is that not asking altogether too much?

(*A.*): To take your last question first, the memory of past persecutions: surely you do not suggest that resentment should be kept rankling and old hatreds perpetuated? It is, of course, never an easy thing to break with the past, to cast off traditions and memories. But millions of American immigrants have done just that without great effort. And if we accept the fact that anti-Semitism is not a transient phenomenon, then this sacrifice imposes itself to a much higher degree in the case of the Jews than, say, in the case of Italian emigrants to the United States. While the Italians are fleeing from poverty alone, the Jews must get away from the spectre of extermination. It is imperative that the Jews should face up to their responsibilities to their children, whatever the wrench to their own feelings.

(*Q.*): Do you not think that the best, the most reasonable and most honourable policy for the Diaspora Jew is to carry on as in the past and at the same time to help build up the State of Israel as an eventual haven of refuge in a minority-baiting world?

(*A.*): No. That is the Jewish tragedy of wanting to have the cake and to eat it at the same time. That way lies disaster.

(*Q.*): Do you believe that Israel, as you say in your Epilogue to *Promise and Fulfilment*, is now so "firmly established" that it can get along without further aid from the Diaspora? Is not your cry "Israel or renunciation" altogether premature, for even supposing that five million Galut Jews were to opt instantly for "next year in Jerusalem," there just would not be any room for them there?

(*A.*): Israel is no less firmly established to-day than any European country which lives under the Communist menace. In view of the magnitude of the problem which Israel is facing in the absorption of immigrants, I would suggest that for a limited period of, say, five years, world Jewry should be encouraged to help finance the settlement of those Jews who desire, or are obliged, to migrate to Israel. After this transition period, there should no longer be any Zionist Organisation of America, no United Jewish Appeal, no Zionist movement, no fund-raising, in fact none of this paradox of a State proud of its sovereignty and yet going round with the begging-bowl.

As for your hypothesis of five million Jews wanting to go to Israel straight away, that is pure fantasy. The bulk of Jewry is in America. But only a few hundred American Jews have moved to Israel since its foundation. It would actually be a splendid thing for Israel if 50,000 American Jews with the right qualifications could be persuaded to go out at once. With their Western culture and technical ability they would transform Israel, and they would be ten times more valuable now than in the future.

(*Q.*): Do you still regard yourself as a Jew? Do you wish others to consider you as being no longer a Jew?

(*A.*): Insofar as religion is concerned, I consider the Ten Commandments and the Sermon on the Mount as inseparable as the root and the flower. Insofar as race is concerned, I have no idea and take no interest in the question how many Hebrews, Babylonians, Roman legionaries, Christian crusaders, and Hungarian nomads were among my ancestors. I consider it a chance occurrence that my father happened to be of the Jewish faith; but I felt that it committed me morally to identify myself with the Zionist movement, as long as there was no haven for the persecuted and the homeless. The moment that Israel became a reality I felt released from this commitment, and free to choose between becoming an Israelite in Israel or a European in Europe. My whole development and cultural allegiance made Europe the natural choice. Hence, to give a precise answer to your question: I regard myself first as a member of the European community, secondly as a naturalised British citizen of uncertain and mixed racial origin, who accepts the ethical values and rejects the dogmas of our Heleno-Judæo-Christian tradition. Into what pigeon-hole others put me is their affair.

That was the end of this long interview, followed by Mr. Carr's conclusion:

I do fear that a large number of lukewarm Jews are subconsciously thinking along the lines formulated by Arthur Koestler; and his "thinking aloud" on their behalf may prove extremely useful in drawing attention to an, as it were, submerged menace.

4

The publication of this interview aroused general indignation among the *Jewish Chronicle's* readers. The protests were headed by a letter from the President of the Anglo-Jewish Association, the Hon. Ewen E. S. Montague, o.b.e., k.c., which was a beautiful example of question-begging :

The brilliantly written interview by Mr. Maurice Carr, in which the apostasy from Judaism of Mr. Koestler is reported, will have filled most of your readers with distress and dismay. . . .

Mr. Koestler . . . has sought to justify his action by stating that there are now only two courses that a Jew can take: to emigrate to Israel or to abandon his religion.

Many Jews have decided, or will decide, to take the former course, with the full respect, sympathy, and understanding, as well as the good wishes, of their respective communities. But why should the thousands of others have to take the second course—the one adopted by Mr. Koestler?

The Anglo-Jewish Association numbers among its members many devout Jews of a piety that can be assailed by no one; they, in common with all our other members, find no difficulty in the present circumstances in reconciling Judaism, and an earnest and sincere wish that Israel may prosper, with a pride in their British citizenship and a full share in the duties, obligations, and rights of that status.

. . . It is vital, at this time in particular, to ensure that no one can doubt that one can still be a sincere Jew and a loyal citizen of the country in which he is living.

Together with the President of the Anglo-Jewish Association's letter, the paper printed another protest by a reader who declared in one paragraph:

Assimilation . . . solves nothing. The fault, dear Mr. Koestler, lies not in the Jews themselves, but in the intolerence of the people living around them. . . .

—and continued a few lines further on:

The Jew trying to assimilate is to me a pitiable figure lacking in sincerity. . . .

A week later the journal came out with an editorial:

The very provocative interview, published recently in *The Jewish Chronicle*, with Mr. Arthur Koestler, should remind us of the fact, apparent to most Jewish women, that the home is the citadel in which to defend the Jewish faith . . . And there has yet to be found any comparable system of daily home life. The dietary laws receive daily confirmation from leading medical authorities: the Jewish housewife down the ages knew how often they protected her and her loved ones from the scourges and plagues that raged around her. Is she, then, at a time when the world so badly needs good men and women, to abandon her faith and sink her own and her family's identity, in order that boys and girls may appear like robots in uniforms indistinguishable one from another?

Still in the same issue there were more letters of protest, all of them sadly illustrative of the manner in which religious fervour degenerates, unnoticed by the believer, into racial pride and perpetual resentment:

In common with the vast majority of my fellow-Jews, outside as well as inside Israel, I feel myself to be just one of a grand array of comrades-in-arms, clad in spiritual armour, scattered over the wide world, and engaged in a fierce and enduring defensive action for a world of freedom, truth, and justice. This struggle began on the day about 4,000 years ago, when the Children of Israel turned their backs on the slave-State of Egypt. . . . More than a thousand years ago a Hebrew poet or *paitan* gave us the answer in *Vehi She'amda*, that beautiful jewel embedded in the Hagada: "This it is which has stood by our fathers and ourselves. For not one enemy alone has risen up against us to destroy us, but in every generation they rise up against us to destroy us, but the Holy One, blessed be He, delivers us from out of their hands" . . . Mr. Koestler seems to be unaware of the fact that the Sermon on the Mount has its origin in Rabbinic thought, that it is merely a rehash of Jewish doctrine. . . . Why does not Mr. Koestler turn his brilliant pen to a far nobler purpose? Let him fight, and urge others to fight, against intolerance and injustice, but let him not ask us obsequiously to crawl to our oppressors' camp, where these two evils have flourished for so long.

Another week later the paper came out with yet another editorial:

> In actual fact, the dilemma which Mr. Koestler poses . . . is basically false. . . . While the Holy Land must always retain its unique significance for Jewry, the message of Judaism and the mission of the Jewish people are not confined to the Holy Land but are universalistic in character. . . . the undying Messianic hopes and aspirations of our Faith forbid us to withdraw from our world-wide mission in the service of mankind. More than ever in these days are we called upon to promote, in whatever country we may dwell, the Jewish ideals of righteousness and brotherhood among the nations. It is not easy to share Mr. Koestler's satisfaction that modern civilisation stands in no need of this Jewish contribution.

Apparently the official organ of British Jewry still regards "the ideal of righteousness and brotherhood" as a Jewish monopoly; it actually drove its message home with the somewhat dated quotation: "and ye shall be unto Me a kingdom of priests and a holy nation." If the paper's claim were to be taken seriously, it would mean that Messrs. Ben Gurion and Mendès-France, Comrade Kaganovich and Henry Morgenthau, Albert Einstein and Louis B. Mayer of Metro-Goldwyn-Mayer, are all commonly engaged in carrying out a specifically Jewish mission. It is precisely this kind of turgid bombast which gave rise to the legend of the Elders of Zion and keeps suspicions of a Jewish world-conspiracy alive. But the controversy served nevertheless a useful purpose by letting the cat of fierce racial pride out of the religious bag, and revealing the tragic contradiction of Jewish existence. For how is the world to reconcile the claim that an Englishman of Jewish faith is like other Englishmen, with the statement, printed in the same issue of the paper: "To be a Jew means that you believe that the past of Jewry is your past, its present your present, its future your future"?

It is remarkable that England's leading Jewish paper did not receive or print a single letter of even partial support for assimilation—which after all has been going on as a historic process for a few thousand years. The passages that I have quoted give only a feeble taste of the vehemence and abuse which the interview aroused in this, probably the most liberal, tolerant and enlightened Jewish community in the world. One can understand the true believer who exclaims with John Donne: "Oh, for some, not to be martyrs is a martyrdom." But to protest against martyrdom and yet ask for just a little more of it for one's children and children's children without knowing why, is a less defensible attitude.

5

I shall now elaborate some of the points raised in the controversy, and shall at the same time try to progress from abstract argument to the field of practical measures. It will be simplest to resort to the form of the imaginary dialogue (which in this case is based on a series of actual dialogues in the past):

(*Question*): All previous attempts of Jewish communities to become completely assimilated to their host nation have ended in failure—see Germany for instance; why should it be different this time?

(*Answer*): The reason for past failures and tragedies is that so far all attempts at assimilation were half-hearted, based on the faulty assumption that the Jews could become full-blooded members of their host nations while retaining their religion and remaining the Chosen Race. *Ethnic assimilation is impossible while maintaining the Mosaic faith; and the Mosaic faith becomes untenable with ethnic assimilation.* The Jewish religion perpetuates national separateness—there is no way around that fact.

There is, on the other hand, at least one example of successful assimilation on a large scale: the Spanish Jews, who some five centuries ago embraced the Catholic faith as an alternative to expulsion, and who (with the exception of a heroically stubborn minority who continued to practise Judaism in secret until they were martyred) have been completely absorbed, racially and culturally, by the Spaniards. To quote Toynbee again: "There is every reason to believe that in Spain and Portugal to-day there is a strong tincture of the blood of these Jewish converts in Iberian veins, especially in the upper and middle classes. Yet the most acute psycho-analyst would find it difficult, if samples of living upper- and middle-class Spanish and Portuguese were presented to him, to detect those who had Jewish ancestors."

(Q.): Your arguments are based on the assumption that the only, or at least the principal, distinguishing mark of the Jew is his religion. What about race, physical features, and those peculiarities of Jewish character and behaviour which are difficult to define and yet easy to sense?

(A.): Racial anthropology is a controversial and muddy field, but there is a kind of minimum agreement among anthropologists on at least these two points: (a) that the Biblical tribe belonged to the Mediterranean branch of the Caucasian race, and (b) that the motley mass of individuals spread all over the world and designated as "Jews" are from the racial point of view an extremely mixed group who have only a remote connection, and in many cases no connection at all, with that tribe.

The contrast between the short, wiry, dark-skinned Yemenite Jew who looks like an Arab, and his Scandinavian co-religionist is obvious. Less well-known is the fact that even Jews from geographically close neighbourhoods (e.g. Russian and Polish Jews) differ markedly in physical type. Certain Italian and Spanish physiognomies are pronouncedly semitic in appearance, and some Spanish families have probably a higher percentage of semitic genes than those groups of European Jews whose ancestors got into the way of the Crusaders and other marauding hordes. But the most puzzling racial paradox of all is the quite un-Jewish appearance and mentality of the new native generation in Israel:

> The Palestine-born young Jew's nickname, *sabra*, is derived from the prickly, wild-growing, somewhat tasteless fruit of the cactus plant. In physical appearance he is invariably taller than his parents, robustly built, mostly blond or brown-haired, frequently snub-nosed and blue-eyed. The young male's most striking feature is that he looks entirely un-Jewish; even his movements are angular and abrupt in contrast to the characteristic curvy roundedness of "Jewish" gestures. The girls, on the other hand, seem as yet to remain physically closer to the Eastern-European Jewish type. On the whole, there can be little doubt that the race is undergoing some curious biological alteration, probably induced by the abrupt change in climate, diet and the mineral balance of the soil. It also seems that the female is slower in undergoing this transformation, more inert or stable in constitutional type. The whole phenomenon confirms in a striking manner that environment has a greater formative influence than heredity, and that what we commonly regard as Jewish characteristics are not racial features, but a product of sustained social pressures and a specific way of life, a psycho-somatic response to "the stimulus of penalisations".

In his mental make-up the average young *sabra* is fearless to the point of recklessness, bold, extroverted and little inclined towards, if not openly contemptuous of, intellectual pursuits. The children are particularly good-looking; after puberty however, their features and voices coarsen and seem never quite to reach the balance of maturity. The typical *sabra*'s face has something unfinished about it; the still undetermined character of a race in transition. His diction is abrupt and unmodulated, which sometimes gives the impression of rudeness. . . . What kind of civilisation he will produce one cannot foretell, but one thing seems fairly certain: within a generation or two Israel will have become an entirely "un-Jewish" country. (*Promise and Fulfilment*, 1949.)

When the fallacies of racialism have been discarded, all that survives of the Biblical race is probably a statistically very small "hard core" of genes which, in certain segregated, intermarrying Jewish communities kept "Mendling out", as the biologist says, in curved noses and wistful irises. But even regarding such facial features it is extremely difficult to distinguish between true heredity and environmental influence. The fairly uniform facial changes of priests living in celibacy, of actors, of convicts serving long sentences, and other types of "professional physiognomies" could easily be mistaken for racial characteristics; and the growing likeness of ageing married couples is an equally puzzling confirmation of the feature-forming power of shared environment.

Turning from physical appearance to the mental habits and peculiarities of Jews, these vary so widely from country to country that we can only regard them as the product of social, not biological inheritance. The typical Jewish abhorrence of drunkenness, for instance, is the unconscious residue of living for centuries under precarious conditions which made it dangerous to lower one's guards; the Jew with the yellow star on his back had to remain cautious and sober, and watch with amused or frightened contempt the antics of the drunken Goy. Revulsion against alcohol and any other form of excess, recklessness and debauch, was instilled from parent to child in successive generations—down to the milk-drinking Prime Minister of France and the abstemious owners of Château-Laffitte.

Jewish casuistry, hair-splitting and logic-chopping, can be traced back to the Talmudic exercises which, until quite recently, dominated the Jewish child's curriculum in school; as one brilliant biographer of Marx has pointed out, the Dialectic owes as much to Hegel as to Marx's rabbinical background.* The financial and forensic genius of the Jew is obviously a consequence of the fact that until the end of the eighteenth century, and in some countries well into the nineteenth, Jews were debarred from most normal professions; the reasons why in the arts and letters Jews play an interpretative rather than a creative part, has been exhaustively analysed in Isaiah Berlin's essay.

We thus have a small and somewhat hypothetical "hard core" of Jewish characteristics in the sense of biological heredity, and a vast complex of physical and mental characteristics which are of environmental origin and transmitted through social inheritance. Both the biological and social features are too complex and diffuse to identify the Jew as a Jew with anything approaching certainty; the decisive test and official identification mark remains his religion.

(Q.): Your arguments may be logical, but it is nevertheless inhuman to ask people to discard, in the name of expediency, a centuries-old tradition as if it were a worthless garment.

(A.): Let us try to define what exactly we mean by "Jewish tradition". Do we mean the concept of monotheism, the enthronement of the one and invisible God, the ethos of the Hebrew

---

* Leopold Schwarzschild, *The Red Prussian*, London, 1948.

prophets, the wisdom of Solomon, the Book of Job? They are all in the King James's Bible and have become the common property of the Western world. *Whatever came after the Bible is either not specifically Jewish, or not part of a living tradition.* Since the conquest of Jerusalem by Titus A.D. 71, the Jews have ceased to be a nation, and ceased to have a language and secular culture of their own. Hebrew as a spoken language went out of use long before the beginning of the Christian era (at the time of Jesus, the language of Palestine was Aramaic); the Jewish scholars and poets in Spain wrote in Arabic, as their descendants wrote in Italian, German, English, French, Polish and Russian. It is true that certain segregated Jewish communities developed a vernacular or *patois* of their own, such as Sephardi and Yiddish, but none of these produced a literature of any consequence and even remotely comparable to the imposing "Jewish" contribution to German, Austrian, English or American culture.

The only specifically Jewish intellectual activity of the post-Biblical centuries was theological. But Talmud, and Kabbala, and the endless volumes of rabbinical exegesis are unknown to 99 per cent. of the general Jewish public, and are no more part of a living tradition than the exercises in casuistry of the medieval Schoolmen. Yet they were the *only* product of a specifically "Jewish tradition", if that expression is to be given concrete meaning, during the last two thousand years.

In other words: since the first century A.D. the Jews have had no national history, no language, literature and culture of their own. Their philosophical, scientific and artistic achievements consist in contributions to the culture of their host nations; they do not constitute a common cultural inheritance or autonomous body of traditions. The fallacy of postulating a special Jewish "mission" and "tradition" becomes evident if we consider that in these terms Disraeli was part of the mission, Gladstone was not, Trotsky was part of it, Lenin was not; Freud was, Jung is not;

and that Jewish readers ought to prefer Proust to Joyce, Kafka to Poe, because the first in each pair is part of the tradition, the second is not.

To sum up: the Jews of our day have no cultural tradition in common, merely certain habits and behaviour-patterns, derived from a religion whose commandments they reject, and from the unhealthy environmental pressures on a segregated minority. The sooner all this is discarded, together with segregation and minority status, the better for all concerned.

(Q.): More logic-chopping. You carve up that indefinable entity "tradition" into tidy categories as if it were a steak that you can cut into chunks. But when a Jew, even a hundred per cent. agnostic American, hears the ancient injunction: "Hark O Israel: the Lord our God, the Lord is one", then something stirs in him which makes all your arguments collapse.

(A.): That something that stirs in him is shared by all mankind. I reject the arrogant presumption of your witness who believes that the message is addressed to him and his kin alone. That, if you permit me to say so, is a metaphysical snobbery based on genealogical assumptions as untenable as Houston Stewart Chamberlain's myth of the Nordic Man.

(Q.): You are very impatient with Jewish emotionalism, but there are other minorities just as sentimental and tradition-bound—think, for instance, of the Irish Catholics in the United States.

(A.): The parallel is misleading. The Irish-American's ties to his old country date from a recent past and fade away in the second or third generation. The Jew's "old country" is not the country of his parents or grandparents, but of a hypothetical ancestor who abandoned it two thousand years ago. The American Jew's sentimental allegiance to the State of Israel is not of the same kind as e.g. the Italo-American's feeling for Italy. Italo-Americans *come* from Italy. Jewish-Americans do not come from Israel but long to go there—or at least pretend to in their prayers.

There is a very serious practical problem involved in this. In both World Wars, Americans of German, Italian and Japanese descent fought in the American Army against their countries of origin. They had become assimilated and detached from their ancestral ties; whereas the Englishman or American who persists in regarding himself as a Jew by religion and tradition, remains attached to the State of Israel both in a mystical and a directly political manner. The imputation of "split loyalties" is an old anti-semitic argument. The existence of the State of Israel and of the international Zionist organisation lends this imputation a measure of reality fraught with danger. I do not mean danger to England or America, but to the Jews themselves. Israel is no longer a mystic promise, but an independent state with an independent policy, and any political allegiance to a foreign country is bound to arouse suspicion in times of international crisis. The results to which such suspicions may lead we know only too well from the past.

(Q.): Even if all your arguments were granted, there would still remain a deep-felt reluctance, a spiritual and æsthetic revulsion in Jewish parents against the idea of bringing up their children in a faith in which they themselves do not believe.

(A.): My plea is addressed to parents who do not believe in the Jewish religion either; to that vast majority of agnostics and near-agnostics who accept the ethical values of our Judeo-Christian heritage and reject all rigid doctrine. The educational system in most countries requires that a child, on entering school, should receive religious instruction. The decision whether he will be instructed in Catholic, Protestant or Jewish dogma is not the child's, but depends on the hazard of his parents' denomination. The proper thing for parents who reject all dogma is to say: "If my child must be brought up in a definite religion, then let it be the same in which his playmates are brought up, and not one which sets him apart by its archaic racial doctrine, marks him out as a scapegoat, and gives him mental complexes. Which particular doctrine he is taught does not matter very much, as with maturity he will make his own spiritual decisions anyway; what matters is that he should not start under a handicap."

(Q.): Your arguments betray a utilitarian approach to religious questions which seems to me cynical and improper.

(A.): Only because you suffer from the guilt-complex of the agnostic who is unable to hold a dogmatic belief but wishes that he could. That, I suspect, goes for all of us, children of the post-materialistic era, filled with transcendental yearnings; once more conscious of a higher, extra-sensory order of reality, and yet intellectually too honest to accept any dogmatic version of it as authentic. If you belong to this category, then surely you too regard the historical accounts of the lives of Buddha, Moses, Jesus and Mohammed as eternal symbols, as archetypes of man's transcendental experience and spiritual aspirations, and it makes little difference which set of symbols will be taught to your child according to the hazard of his birth. In my personal opinion it is essential for the moral development of the child to start with some form of belief in a divine order, whose framework he will at first take for Gospel truth until the spiritual content matures into symbolic interpretation. From this point of view—which is the basis of our discussion since my argument is expressly *not* directed at the orthodox believer—it is quite irrelevant whether the child's imagination is centred on Moses bringing water forth from the rock or on the miracle of the water turned into wine at Cana.

Allow me to reverse the charge: I find it cynical on your part to turn your child into a potential victim by teaching him to believe in the miracle of the rock but not in the miracle of Cana, or by celebrating the Sabbath on Saturday instead of Sunday. Do you realise that this futile calendrical dispute, the Jew closing

his shop on Saturday and working on Sunday, has been a major
irritant and cause of martyrdom for countless centuries? Do you
call it cynical if one deplores the holocausts of Jewish victims
burnt, raped, robbed, chased and gassed in the name of a Lilli-
putian fanaticism regarding the question on which end to break
the spiritual egg?

(Q.): Let us turn to the practical side of the problem. You
advocate that non-doctrinaire Jews should bring up their children
as members of the congregation of their neighbours; what about
"restricted" residential districts and schools, and similar obstacles,
handicaps and embarrassments?

(A.): No doubt in the first generation there will be plenty of
all that, plenty of bitterness, disappointment and failure in individual cases. But in the second generation there will be less of it,
and in the third, what with intermarriage and the disappearance
of all self-segregatory motives, the "Jewish question" will gradually taper off and fade away. The obvious example of this process
is the cultural and social homogeneity of third-generation Americans of heterogeneous origin. Immigrants of the first generation
have a natural tendency to huddle together with their country-
men and to show suspicion and hostility to other groups; the
second generation, once through American school, has an equally
natural tendency to break away from parental traditions, to cast off
their distinguishing marks, and become full-fledged Americans.
The Jews alone among the varied European immigrant population have resisted this "tapering off" process, and persist in
their religious, social and ethnic separateness generation after
generation.

I repeat that in the past there were good excuses for this.
Before the resurrection of Israel, to renounce Jewry meant to
deny solidarity with the persecuted, and might have been regarded
as a cowardly capitulation. The Jews could not vanish from the
scene of history in an anti-climax. But with the rebirth of the

Jewish State, the climax is reached, the circle is closed. It is no longer a question of capitulation, but of a free choice. Hence the obligation for Jewry to pause on its long journey, review its situation and face the facts which some time ago it was excusable and even honourable to shun.

6

I shall now have to deal with one last objection which carries more psychological weight than all the others, because it is not based on logic but on the denial of logic as a guide in human affairs. Isaiah Berlin has expressed this attitude with much insight and eloquence in his essay. After explaining that he was to a large extent in agreement with my position, Mr. Berlin continued with a "but":

> But there are . . . many individuals in the world who do not choose to see life in the form of radical choices between one course and another, and whom we do not condemn for this reason. "Out of the crooked timber of humanity" said a great philosopher, "no straight thing was ever made." Fearful thinkers, with minds seeking salvation in religious or political dogma, souls filled with terror, may wish to eliminate such ambiguous elements in favour of a more clear-cut structure, and they are, in this respect, true children of the new age which with its totalitarian systems has tried to institute just such an order among human beings, and sort them out neatly each to his own category. . . . To protest about a section of the population merely because it is felt to be an uncosy element in society, to order it to alter its outlook or get out . . . is . . . a kind of petty tyranny, and derives ultimately from the conviction that human beings have no right to behave foolishly or inconsistently or vulgarly, and that society has the right to try and rid

itself by humane means, but rid itself nevertheless, of such persons although they are neither criminals nor lunatics nor in any sense a danger to the lives or liberties of their fellows. This attitude, which is sometimes found to colour the views of otherwise civilised and sensitive thinkers, is a bad attitude because it is clearly not compatible with the survival of the sort of reasonable, humane, "open", social texture in which human beings can enjoy those freedoms and those personal relationships upon which all tolerable life depends.

Mr. Berlin is as sceptical as I am regarding the possibility of normalising the social status of Jews so long as they insist on calling themselves and being called Jews. Half of his essay is devoted to a penetrating analysis of the psychological factors inherent in the Jewish condition which make anti-semitism, past, present and future, unavoidable. He also agrees that the rebirth of the State of Israel puts every individual Jew in a dilemma. His argument is simply that you should neither expect nor encourage people to act logically, and that unreason, however irritating or maddening, must be tolerated.

I fully agree that nothing could be more unreasonable than to expect people to behave reasonably. But if you argue that Jews have a right to be guided by irrational emotion and to behave "foolishly, or inconsistently, or vulgarly", you must grant the same right to their adversaries, and I need not quote you the result. It seems to me that if you have a voice and a pen, it is incumbent on you to advocate that course of action which you believe to be in the public interest, and thereby to influence the precarious balance between reason and passion in people's minds. It also seems to me, as I said before, that people have an inalienable right to mess up their own lives, but no right to mess up the lives of their children, just because being a Jew is such a cosy mess. The pressure of totalitarian forces from outside and inside our Western civilisation has led to a tendency among liberals like Mr. Berlin to call any attitude of non-complacency "totalitarian". If you try to sort out logically a complex situation and to point out that it demands a choice between alternative lines of action, you will promptly be accused of painting in black-and-white. A certain amount of administrative and ideological muddle, a margin of tolerated confusion are indeed as essential to the functioning of a democratic society as lubricants and safety valves are to a machine. But the harsh, inhuman precision of totalitarian ideologies makes the liberal mind inclined to believe that the safety valves are all that matter, whereas pistons, pressure and energy are totalitarian as such. Words like "blueprint", "planning", and even "order" have acquired a derogatory meaning ever since various forms of a "new order" were looming on the horizon. The understandable human weakness for evading painful decisions and responsibilities has come to be regarded as a virtue and the essence of democracy. The liberal in retreat does not ask for freedom of choice, but for freedom from choice.

If my saying that we must decide whether we belong to the Chosen Race or to the nation whose citizen we are, if the revolutionary discovery that we can't eat our cake and have it, are figments of a totalitarian mind, then I must confess to a totalitarian mind. If "out of the crooked timber of humanity no straight thing was ever made", I still think it more honourable to try to straighten the timber than to make it more crooked for sweet crookedness' sake. Or shall we rather fall back on the ancient adage:

> *When in danger or in doubt,*
> *Turn in circles, scream or shout?*

7

In summing up, I may be allowed to quote from the closing page of *Promise and Fulfilment:*

Orthodox Jewry is a vanishing minority. It is the well-meaning but confused majority which, through inertia, perpetuates the anachronism by clinging to a tradition in which it no longer really believes, to a mission which is fulfilled, a pride which has become inverted cowardice. Let them stop to think whether they have the right to place the burden of the ominous knapsack, now void of contents, on their children who have not asked for it.

To break the vicious circle of being persecuted for being "different", and being "different" by force of persecution, they must arrive at a clear decision, however difficult this may be. They must either follow the imperative of their religion, the return to the Promised Land—or recognise that that faith is no longer theirs. To renounce the Jewish faith does not mean to jettison the perennial values of Judaic tradition. Its essential teachings have passed long ago into the mainstream of the Judeo-Christian heritage. If a Judaic religion is to survive outside Israel, without inflicting the stigma of separateness on its followers and laying them open to the charge of divided loyalties, it would have to be a system of faith and cosmopolitan ethics freed from all racial presumption and national exclusivity. But a Jewish religion thus reformed would be stripped of its specifically Jewish content.

These conclusions, reached by one who has been a supporter of the Zionist Movement for a quarter-century, while his cultural allegiance belonged to Western Europe, are mainly addressed to the many others in a similar situation. They have done what they could to help to secure a haven for the homeless in the teeth of prejudice, violence and political treachery. Now that the State of Israel is firmly established, they are at last free to do what they could not do before: to wish it good luck and go their own way with the nation whose life and culture they share, without reservation or split loyalties.

The mission of the Wandering Jew is completed; he must discard the knapsack and cease to be an accomplice in his own destruction. The fumes of the death chambers still linger over Europe; there must be an end to every calvary.

The Boredom of Fantasy

Broadcast on the BBC Home Service, May, 1953

ONCE UPON a time, more precisely on the 17th June, A.D. 4784, Captain Kayle Clark stepped into a public telescreen box to call up his fiancée, secret agent Lucy Rall. He was told that Lucy was not available as she had got married a week before. "To whom?" cried the exasperated Captain. "To me," said the man to whom he was talking. Taking a closer look at the telescreen, the Captain discovered with a mild surprise that the man he was talking to was himself.

The startling mystery was solved by Mr. Robert Headrock, the first immortal man on earth. Headrock, using his electronic super-brain computer, discovered that Captain Clark had taken a trip in a time-machine; that he had made a loop into the past, and married Lucy Rall without his unlooped present self knowing about it. Through this little frolic, he also became the richest man on earth as he knew the movements of the Stock Exchange in advance. When the point in time was reached where Clark had looped off in the time-machine, the past Clark and the present Clark became again one, and lived happily ever after. Meanwhile, Robert Headrock, the immortal man, sent a journalist called MacAllister several million trillion years back into the past and made him cause a cosmic explosion, which gave rise to our planetary system as we know it.

The Boredom of Fantasy

The book from which I was quoting is called *The Weapon Shops of Isher* by A. E. van Vogt. Mr. van Vogt is probably the most popular of contemporary American science-fiction writers. The book was recently published in England in a science-fiction series which signals, together with the founding of the British Science-Fiction Club, that the new craze, a kind of cosmic jitterbug, has crossed the Atlantic.

I had better confess at this point that while I lived in the United States I was a science-fiction addict myself and am still liable to occasional relapses. Reading about space travel, time travel, Martian maidens, robot civilisations and extra-galactic supermen is habit-forming like opium, murder thrillers and yoghourt diets. Few people in this country realise the extent and virulence of this addiction in the United States. According to a recent survey, the average sale of a detective story or a Western thriller in America is four thousand copies; the average sale of a science-fiction novel is six thousand copies, or fifty per cent. higher. Every month, six new novels of this type are published in the U.S.A. and three large publishing firms specialise exclusively in science-fiction. There is a flood of science-fiction magazines, science-fiction clubs, science-fiction films, television programmes and so on. The addicts are called "fen", which is the plural of fan. Fen gather in clubhouses called slanshacks, "slan" meaning a biologically mutated superman, and hold conferences, called fenferences. The characters in science-fiction speak a kind of cosmic R.A.F. slang (it ought to be called, evidently, "cosmi-lingo"). Young space cadets, for instance, dislike meeting Bems— for bug-eyed Monsters—in alien galaxies unless armed with paraguns—paralysis-causing rayguns. They swear "By space", "By the seven rings of Saturn", or "By the gas-pits of Venus".

If grown-ups betray these strange symptoms, one can imagine how the kiddies react. Your friends' children no longer plug you with six-shooters; they atomise you with nuclear blasters. They wear plastic bubbles around their heads which look like divers' helmets and enable them to breathe while floating in gravity-free interstellar space. These are sold by the thousand in department stores together with other cosmic paraphernalia, and are steadily replacing cowboy equipment, just as on the television screen Tom Corbett, Space Cadet, is in the process of replacing Hopalong Cassidy as the children's national hero. Even the housewife, listening in to the radio while on her domestic chores, is becoming cosmic-minded. The soap opera has branched out into the space opera. Imagine the opposite number of Mrs. Dale in Texas or Minnesota: "I am so worried about Richard not being back from his luncheon date on Jupiter. Maybe he's got space-happy and gone on to Venus. Or one of those nasty meteors may have deflected him from his orbit."

So much for the grotesque side of science-fiction. But a craze of such vast dimensions is never entirely crazy. It always expresses, in a distorted way, some unconscious need of the time. Science-fiction is a typical product of the atomic age. The discoveries of that age weigh like an undigested lump on the stomach of mankind. Electronic brains which predict election results, lie-detectors which make you confess the truth, new drugs which make you testify to lies, radiations which produce biological monsters—all these developments of the last fifty years have created new vistas and new nightmares, which art and literature have not yet assimilated. In a crude and fumbling fashion, science-fiction is trying to fill this gap. But there is perhaps another and more hidden reason for this sudden hunger for other ages and other worlds. Perhaps, when they read about the latest hydrogen bomb tests, people are more aware than they admit to themselves, of the possibility that human civilisation may be approaching its end. And together with this may go a dim, inarticulate suspicion that the cause lies deeper than Communism or Fascism, that it may lie in the nature itself of *homo sapiens*; in other words, that the human race may be a biological misfit doomed to extinction like the giant reptiles of an earlier age. I believe that some apocalyptic intuition of this kind may be one of the reasons for the sudden interest in life on other stars.

As a branch of literature, science-fiction is, of course, not new. As early as the second century Lucian, a Greek writer, wrote a story of a journey to the moon. Swift wrote science-fiction; so did Samuel Butler, Jules Verne, H. G. Wells, Aldous Huxley, George Orwell. But while in the past such exercises were isolated literary extravaganzas, they are now mass-produced for a mass audience. Moreover, modern science-fiction takes itself very seriously. There are certain rules of the game which every practitioner must observe, otherwise he will be torn to shreds by the critics. The basic rule is that the author may only operate with future inventions, gadgets and machines which are extrapolations (that is, logical extensions) of present discoveries, and do not go against the laws of nature. A number of physicists, doctors and biologists are employed by the film and television industries to make sure that, even in the childrens' science-fiction show, every detail is correct. Some of the best-known science-fiction authors in America are actually scientists, several of international repute, who write under pen-names. The most recent and distinguished recruit to their ranks is Lord Russell. All this is a guarantee of scientific accuracy, but unfortunately not of artistic quality.

Mr. Gerald Heard has recently expressed the opinion that science-fiction is "the mark of the dawn of a new vision, and the rise of a new art", and simply *the* future form of the novel. Other well-known critics overseas also believe, in all seriousness, that science-fiction, now in its infancy, will grow up and one day become the literature of the future.

I do not share their opinion. I believe that science-fiction is good entertainment, and that it will never become good art. It is reasonably certain that within the next hundred years we shall have space-travel, but at that stage the description of a trip to the moon will no longer be science-fiction but simple reportage. It will be fact, not fantasy, and the science-fiction of that time will have to go even further to startle the reader. What Mr. Heard's claim really amounts to is the replacement of the artist's disciplined imagination by the schoolboy's unbridled fantasy. But day-dreaming is not poetry, and fantasy is not art.

At first sight one would of course expect that imaginative descriptions of non-human societies on alien planets would open new vistas for the somewhat stagnant novel of our time. But most disappointingly this is not the case, and for a simple reason. Our imagination is limited; we cannot project ourselves into the distant future any more than into the distant past. This is the reason why the historical novel is practically dead to-day. The life of an Egyptian civil servant under the Eighteenth Dynasty, or even of a soldier in Cromwell's army, is only imaginable to us in dim outline; we are unable to identify ourselves with the strange figure moving through such a strange world. Few Englishmen can really understand the feelings and habits of Frenchmen, much less of Russians, much less of Martians. And without this act of identification, of intimate understanding, there is no art, only a thrill of curiosity which soon yields to boredom. The Martian heroes of science-fiction may have four eyes, a green skin and an accent stranger than mine—we just couldn't care less. We are tickled by them for a few pages; but because they are too strange to be true, we soon get bored.

For every culture is an island. It communicates with other islands but it is only familiar with itself. And art means seeing the familiar in a new light, seeing tragedy in the trivial event; it means in the last resort broadening and deepening our under-standing of ourselves. Swift's *Gulliver*, Huxley's *Brave New World*, Orwell's *Nineteen-Eighty-Four*, are great works of litera-ture because in them the gadgets of the future and the oddities of alien worlds serve merely as a background or pretext for a social message. In other words, they are literature precisely to the extent to which they are not science-fiction, to which they are works of disciplined imagination and not of unlimited fantasy. A similar rule holds for the detective story. Georges Simenon is probably the greatest master in that field, yet his novels become works of art precisely at the point where character and atmosphere become more important than the plot, where imagination triumphs over invention.

Thus the paradoxical lesson of science-fiction is to teach us modesty. When we reach out for the stars, our limitations become grotesquely apparent. The heroes of science-fiction have unlimited power and fantastic possibilities, but their feelings and thoughts are limited within the narrow human range. Tom Corbett, Space Cadet, behaves on the third planet of Orion exactly in the same way as he does in a drugstore in Minnesota, and one is tempted to ask him: "Was your journey really necessary?" The Milky Way has become simply an extension of Main Street.

Travel is no cure for melancholia; space-ships and time-machines are no escape from the human condition. Let Othello subject Desdemona to a lie-detector test; his jealously will still blind him to the evidence. Let Oedipus triumph over gravity; he won't triumph over his fate.

Some twenty years ago the German writer, Alfred Döblin, wrote a novel in which humanity discovers the secret of biological self-transformation: by a click of their fingers people can change themselves into giants, tigers, demons, or fish—much like Flook in the *DailyMail* cartoon. At the end of the book the last specimens of this happy race sit, each on a solitary rock, in the shape of black ravens, in eternal silence. They have tried, experienced, seen and said everything under the sun, and all that is left for them to do is to die of boredom—the boredom of fantasy.

The Shadow of a Tree

The article which follows may serve as an illustration of the period-bound character of science-fiction. It shows that all Utopias, including horror-Utopias, tell us more about the time when they were written than about the future they purport to predict. I must explain the circumstances which caused it to be written.

In October 1951, Collier's *came out with a special issue of 125 pages, called* Preview of the War We Do Not Want. *The editorial preface declared: "We believe that this is the most important single issue that any magazine has ever published." The issue did in fact create a stir in Europe as hardly any American magazine before, though not in the way it intended.*

From the journalistic point of view it was an unprecedented enterprise. Its preparation took ten months. During that time the contributors were constantly kept informed by the editorial board, of each other's contributions, suggestions and ideas, so that the whole issue assumed a planned and co-ordinated character. The contributors were a team of the strategic, economic and Eastern experts of the New York Times, New York Herald Tribune, Christian Science Monitor; *of radio commentators, authors and politicians, including Hanson Baldwin, Stuart Chase, Marguerite Higgins, Edward Murrow, Professor Allan Nevins, J. B. Priestley, Walter Reuther, Robert Sherwood, Lowell Thomas, Walter Winchell, Philip Wylie, and others.*

The idea behind it all was explained in the editorial, which said:

The Shadow of a Tree

"*We do not think that war is inevitable. We are emphatically*
"*opposed to any suggestion of a 'preventive' war. We believe*
"*that each day of peace and preparation makes the free nations*
"*stronger and lessens the chance of world conflict. Yet such a*
"*conflict could start tomorrow, through design or miscalculation or*
"*desperation. This issue of* Collier's, *written as of* 1960, *shows*
"*how that war would be fought and won, and reports on the pro-*
"*gramme of reconstruction that would follow victory.*

"*We have no illusions about the fearful cost of victory. If the*
"*unwanted war does come, we feel that the peace which follows*
"*should not repeat the pattern of unconditional surrender, repara-*
"*tions and trials of war criminals. The liberated people could be left*
"*to choose the political forms of freedom which would flourish best*
"*in Russian soil.*

"*Implicit in all that you will read in the pages that follow is the*
"*means by which the catastrophe of another war can be avoided.*
"*That means rests with the Soviet government. They can believe*
"*the truth—that the West has no aggressive intentions and is wil-*
"*ling to live at peace with Russia. Or they can continue to delude*
"*their people and themselves with their own propaganda, start a*
"*war, and see enlightenment brought to their people by armed might.*

"*An appeal to the reason of Joseph Stalin and the men around*
"*him is the ultimate purpose of this issue of* Collier's. *And we*
"*earnestly pray that its effect will be to help establish and maintain*
"*an enduring peace.*"

*The issue caused a storm of protest, especially in France—so
much so that the editors hurriedly dropped the project of its repub-
lication in book form. This reaction was typical of the public's
passionate rejection of any warning which brings out people's
repressed fears and compels them to face, if even for an instant,
the hideous and threatening reality around them—(see* A Guide
to Political Neurosis.) *As such bursts of irrational passion must*

always be covered by some rational pretext, the attackers turned the contents of the issue and the intention behind it upside down. The Preview of the War We Do Not Want *was unmistakably intended to act as a warning and deterrent from war; the critics in the French press described it as an encouragement to war and an act of provocation.*

My contribution was meant to outline, from the perspective of 1960, the task of social reconstruction and rehabilitation in post-war Russia. I have no reason to apologise for its content—except for its datedness. 1960 as seen from 1951 was a fundamentally different age from 1960 as seen from 1955. For this piece of Utopia was written in the good old days of the atom bomb, before the hydrogen bomb. Four years ago one could still hope that atomic wars will cause terrible, yet nevertheless limited, damage; and that when the war was over humanity, with a gigantic effort, could find its feet again. To-day this hope no longer exists.

★   ★   ★

THE SHADOW OF A TREE

Our correspondent has recently returned from a three-month journey through Russia. He travelled extensively through the Ukraine, the Moscow region, and was the first correspondent to be admitted to the "Convicts' Republic" (Kolymskaya Respublika Osoozhdyonnykh) on the Kolyma Peninsula in Siberia, about which, since the liberation began, only vague and fantastic rumours have reached the outside world. Mr. Koestler's visit was sponsored by UNIHOPE—the United Nations Housing and Providing Enterprise. The following are edited extracts from his diary. THE EDITORS

Kharkov, 30th June, 1961.

How is one to provide local colour when all the towns in the Ukraine look the same? From the air Kiev, Voronesh, Kharkov, Poltava, seem to have been designed according to one pattern. Near the centre you see two or three huge circular patches; their diameters vary between half a mile and three miles. These patches are the areas of total destruction, which have been cleared and ploughed up by UNIHOPE's flying bulldozer squads and converted into vegetable plots. "Later on" public buildings and parks are supposed to replace them, but this "later on", which is incessantly on every Russian's lips, still belongs to the distant future.

In the past, at any rate, the potatoes and cabbages grown on these plots saved the lives of thousands of citizens in the devastated towns during the famine-years of 1957–8. From the air, the circular potato and cabbage plots look like huge greenish-brown discs. Between and around them sprawl the "old cities" or what remains of them; buildings are propped and patched up by improvised means, windows boarded up for lack of glass and shattered balconies shaved off the scar-faced façades—the whole very dreary and depressing.

Then, outside the "old cities" you see the new quarters of pre-fabricated houses—five, ten, twenty-thousand mass-produced little dwelling cubes, laid out in geometrical patterns by UNIHOPE's building trust. These "Woolworth villages", as æsthetically sensitive visitors call them because they look as if they had been assembled in the Five and Ten Cents Stores, are nevertheless colourful and gay—from the air you get the impression of huge polka-dot ties and ribbons fanning out of the old cities into the surrounding steppe. The living space provided is only sixty square feet per individual, which means that there are two people to a medium-sized room, but for most Russians this is a luxury which they had never known before.

Food and housing were the two nightmare problems which faced the United Nations in liberated Russia. So long as these were not solved, the world "liberation" remained a mockery. The historic achievement of our Atlantic civilisation was not that we won the war, but that we were able *to transform the greatest Army ever known into the greatest welfare organisation ever known*.

The Berlin airlift had proved that the transformation of a destructive force into a providing force was not only technically possible, but also produced quicker results than any philanthropic welfare organisation could achieve. UNIHOPE was an enlargement of the Berlin airlift on a scale of approximately 1,000,000 to 1. The flying Bulldozer Squads, "Operation Harvest", "Operation Vitamin C", and "Operation Housing", saved not only the vanquished Russians; they also saved the victors from the moral disasters which previous wars had brought in their wake. The first World War had been followed by an irresponsible Jazz Age; the second, by half of Europe falling from Hitler's frying pan into Stalin's fire. The third produced UNIHOPE—and restored the shaken self-confidence of our civilisation.

The Shadow of a Tree

Kharkov, July 5th (Election Day)

The elections to the Kharkov Municipal Council—the first free elections since 1917—were a disappointing affair with touches of crude comedy. No fewer than twenty-two parties and "programmes" competed; among them:

The Unified Monarchist Great-Russian Party.
The Ukrainian Separatist Party.
The Peasant Party (individual farmers and small-holders).
The Agrarian Co-operative Party.
The Liberal Democratic Party, and
The Democratic Liberal Party. (The programme of these two parties of the urban middle-classes is indistinguishable, but their leaders are involved in a mortal personal feud.)
The Democratic Workers' Party (free Labour Unionists).
The Syndicalist Workers' Party (followers of Kropotkin's theory of ideal anarchism).
The "Amerikansky Party" (founded by a locally famous black marketeer in the hope of getting on the U.S.A. payroll).
The "Genrik Adamchiki" (Ukrainian spelling of Henry Adamite, founded by a professor who happened to read Adam's work on Progressive Land Taxation).
The Avengers of Trotsky. (This group preaches in a more or less disguised form that Communism was a good thing under Lenin and Trotsky, and only became a bad thing under Stalin. They are a minor headache for our security service.)
The "Kontriky" (former political prisoners and deportees; derived from the abbreviation of "counter-revolutionary element", which was their designation under the Soviet régime. This influential group is held together by a kind of *esprit de corps;* no definite political programme).

These twelve are the "political parties" as we understand the term. The remaining "independent candidates"—cranks, religious sectarians and world reformers—who, since the liberation, are sprouting like mushrooms after rain, might be classed as "religious and miscellaneous". They included:

The Púpils of Tolstoy (a pacifist and vegetarian Christian group, rejecting religious dogmatism).

The Theocrats (followers of the Orthodox church, who hold that Russia should be ruled by the Patriarch Sergei).

The "Old Believers" (a traditionalist sect of religious zealots).

The Servants of God (who refuse to have family names).

The Doukhobor (who refuse to wear clothes).

The Starosti (who preach and sometimes practise self-castration, because mankind is evil and should be brought to an end).

The Esperantists (who hold that introduction of a universal language would solve all problems).

The Pavlovites (who hold that the whole of mankind should be made to have uniform opinions through controlled reconditioning of their reflexes by Professor Pavlov's famous method of training dogs).

The Barankavitzi (have never been able to find out what they want).

The remaining party, called *The World Redeemers*, was founded by an escaped inmate of a mental home, who started raving and had to be locked up on the night before the elections.

In short, Russia is having its exuberant honeymoon with Democracy. The spectacle may seem strange to the Western mind, but I witnessed a similar phenomenon some thirty years ago in Tel Aviv when, during the first municipal election, not less than twenty-four parties were competing for a total of 150,000 votes.

The Shadow of a Tree

There a people was granted political self-determination for the first time in two thousand years; here for the first time in fifty years—provided that we call the Czarist régime a democracy. So it is only natural that after the terrible pressure which they endured, the Russians are having a rollicking time with the new, super-democratic electoral system.

The most remarkable thing about the electoral campaign was its atmosphere of nearly complete calm. Only one or two minor clashes occurred between Monarchists and Separatists. Owing to the shortage of printing facilities, electoral propaganda was in the main confined to hand-printed leaflets, stencilled posters and such-like primitive means. Measured by the standards of American or French electoral campaigns, it was an idyllic affair.

This is probably due to the fact that the man-in-the-street is still unable to take elections seriously. As far back as he can remember, they were a kind of compulsory ritual which resulted in 99·8 per cent. of the population casting its vote for the only existing party. He simply cannot believe that elections have any influence in determining his and the nation's future. What really interests him is the next draw of the Great Lottery, scheduled for the coming Sunday.

Kharkov, July 8th (Wednesday)

The final results of the elections were announced yesterday. They are, to say the least of it, unexpected.

The counting of the votes started with a solemn ceremony in Freedom House, in the presence of the local authorities. The first sealed ballot-box was opened by Colonel Dalcroix who is the local C.O. of UNITOC (United Nations Temporary Occupation Command). Next to him sat Krupnik, Mayor of Kharkov, a broad-faced, impassive man of Ukrainian peasant stock. All went well at the beginning; the Colonel made a short speech, and after the clapping had subsided, pulled the first ballot-paper from the box and handed it solemnly to the Mayor to read the vote. I must explain that each ballot-paper contained a list of the twenty-two parties, each preceded by a little square in which the voter was to mark by a cross the party he had chosen. There was a tense silence, for everybody felt that the first vote had a kind of symbolic significance. Krupnik looked at the paper and announced the vote: "*Da.*"

"*Comment?*" asked the Colonel. "What does he mean by '*da*'?"

"'*Da*' means 'yes'," the translator explained amiably.

"*Mais comment?* For which party did the person vote?"

"The citizen voter voted for them all. He just wrote '*da*' at the top of the paper."

There was a pained silence.

"Well, well," said the Colonel, "let's try the next one." He pulled out a second ballot-paper and handed it to the Mayor.

"*Da,*" Krupnik read impassively.

The female representative of the Peasant party began to giggle; this exploded the tension, and the whole room burst into laughter. Every second or third vote turned out to be a "*da*"; other voters had obediently marked all the twenty-two little squares with crosses. Krupnik continued to read out stolidly the "*da-da's*" with a kind of unconscious approval on his square face. It sounded strangely reassuring, like a child's babbling: "*Da-da-da.*"

The result was announced this morning. The largest number of votes went to the Monarchists and to the Ukrainian Separatists, with the Peasant Party, the former deportees, the Theocrats and the "*Amerikanskys*" as runners-up. Over fifty per cent. of the votes were "*da's*", and had to be invalidated. According to the radio it was the same story everywhere: fifty, sixty, and up to seventy per cent. invalid votes.

The Shadow of a Tree

Dinner at the UNIHOPE canteen with Isakoovich, the translator. He is a wizened little man of fifty, a former school-teacher from Minsk, who lost his whole family in the pogrom-years 1956–7 (the famous Jew-killings organised as a diversion during the Red Army's retreat). He is an intelligent, well-read man, so I was surprised when he said that he had voted for the Pavlovites.

"What do you want?", he said with a shrug. "The elections were the best proof of the truth of Pavlov's theory. You give a dog a series of electric shocks and sound a gong with each shock; after a while the sound of the gong alone will send the dog into convulsions. Similarly, when you speak to a Russian the word 'election' he will twitch with fright and yell '*da*'."

Had I myself made this remark, Isakoovich would have rightly been offended, for he loves Russia; but he spoke with a melancholy detachment. What he said brought home to me that this is an age of science-fiction come true. Not because of the war—on the whole, the war was fought with more conservative weapons than had been previously expected. The fantastic and fascinating novelties are those of mass-psychology. The confessions at the show trials were only a small foretaste of the unholy miracles which a determined modern tyranny can produce by processing the minds of its subjects.

July 10th

Item: Who are the best-paid people, the biggest profiteers in contemporary Russia? The translators of foreign books. When the Curtain rose after forty years, the hunger for books, magazines, for every form of printed material which contained information on the mysterious world in the West was enormous. Nobody wants to read a book by the erstwhile Russian writers; they have for too long played the part of literary prostitutes. The translators, these former pariahs of the arts, have stepped into the shoes of the poets and novelists. Top of the best-seller list is still a Russian translation of the Sears Roebuck catalogue (complete and unabridged) with explanatory footnotes.

Moscow, July 17th

One question that is constantly asked at home is never asked here: "What happened to Communism in Russia?" Everybody yawns when a visitor brings it up, because the answer is so obvious to every Russian. The answer is that there never was Communism in Russia; there were only Communists. When the Communists disappeared, Communism disappeared.

Why is this so self-evident to every Russian, and so difficult to understand for people abroad? Because people outside Russia thought of Soviet Communism as a political system in the Western sense; or as some miscarried attempt to establish social justice; or as a kind of secular religion. It was, of course, nothing of the sort—except for a short period in the beginning, long since forgotten. For the last thirty years—that is, as far back as the memories of the present generation can reach—it had ceased to be a political movement, for it had no opponents in Russia against which it could measure itself in terms of ideas or power. It could not teach the masses any programme or philosophy, for the line changed incessantly in a dizzy zigzag; yesterday's truth became to-day's heresy, and the very foundations of faith and belief were destroyed in the process.

In a primitive community you can sometimes replace political thinking by a kind of simple loyalty to the government. But that loyalty too was destroyed when again and again men who were one day members of the Government confessed the next that they had always been traitors, spies and enemies of the people.

When in the early years of the Revolution the priests vanished from the Russian scene, religion did not vanish with them; it remained alive in the people. But when the Communists vanished from the scene, Communism vanished with them because as a faith it had never existed among the Russian people.

Communism as a faith had, during the last generation, only existed among people outside Russia. It existed because large parts of the population of the world lived in squalor and misery, and wanderers in the desert are always ready to believe in a mirage. The rulers of Russia kept the country hermetically closed to keep up the illusion, and to hide the reality behind the mirage. It was so cunningly done that in the Western world even opponents of the Communist régime had no idea of the full extent of horror which it contained. The truth about Russia was the best kept secret in history.

When I say that Communism in Russia has vanished with the Communists, I do not mean that the results of forty years of indoctrination from the cradle to the grave have vanished with it. The mental ravages caused by that indoctrination are visible at every step here. But that indoctrination did not teach the people Communism. It taught them one word: "*da*". To achieve a 99·8 per cent. unanimous, roaring "*da*" for Comrade Ivan's promotion, and the same roaring "*da*" for his execution; "*da*" for the crusade against the Nazis and "*da*" for the pact with the Nazis; "*da*" for everything which the omniscient leader decided. This task was achieved not by propaganda as we understand it, but by mental processing. The régime did not want Communists; it wanted robots. It will take at least a generation to change the robots back into humans again.

Moscow, July 14th

Three days in bed with 'flu, plagued by *klopy*, the famed Russian bed-bugs. The Russians say it is a new strain of super-*klopy*—a mutation caused by radio-activity, like the red forget-me-not. At any rate, they are formidable beasts and they seem to thrive on DDT.

Being ill I could not attend the drawing of the Lottery, but I am told it was, as always, a huge success, with the usual speeches, concert recitals, dancing, etc. The Lottery is an institution which has come to stay. As people at home seem to have some misconceptions about it, here is a brief history of this most popular feature of contemporary Russian life:

THE STORY OF THE GREAT LOTTERY

Next to food and housing, the third vital post-war problem was the *Bezprizornye*—the locust-plague of waifs and strays turned into juvenile delinquents. These hordes of little savages of every age from seven upward have been a recurrent feature of Soviet life ever since the Revolution. After the Civil War in the early 1920s, their number was estimated at over a million. The mass-deportations in the 'thirties produced new waves of the plague, and the collapse of the Soviet régime led to a resurgence of it on a scale never equalled before. Gangs of juvenile criminals, who had reverted to a stage of primitive savagery, roamed the countryside. Martial law was ineffective against them, for soldiers won't shoot at children. No effective steps could be taken against the black market so long as the racketeers were able to use hordes of corrupted children as their agents and informers. The *Bezprizornye* were the yeast on which crime, drunkenness and prostitution thrived during the famine-years. The most appalling symptom of the plague were the child-brothels, of which Moscow alone counted about a score.

The occupation authorities fought a losing battle against the *Bezprizornye*. They were rounded up, sheltered and fed in improvised camps during the winter of 1956–7. But when spring came, they escaped in droves and swarms from the camps and took to the roads again. The authorities were faced with the loathsome necessity of putting barbed wire, watch towers and armed guards around the children's camps.

The effects of this measure were disastrous. The Soviet régime had deported juvenile delinquents to remote labour camps in Siberia, where they could perish out of sight. The new prison camps for children, which the liberators were forced to establish in the vicinity of every large town from the Black Sea to the Baltic, were sores on their conscience; to Russian eyes they were a hideous reminder of the past, and a proof that the future would be no better. By the autumn of 1957, the number of children in the camps was approaching the one-million mark.

On October 15th, 1957, the "United Nations Commission of Inquiry into Conditions in the Children's Camps in Russia" published its report. It described with complete frankness a situation which was heart-breaking and hair-raising to Western public opinion. In spite of the efforts of a host of pediatricians, psychiatrists, nurses and teachers, the camps were a hotbed of every form of vice and juvenile corruption.The report concluded that no reasonable hope for improvement could be entertained by the forcible herding together of child delinquents behind barbed wire in a desolate country of famine and chaos. The only hope of saving and rehabilitating the children was "to disperse them and transplant them into a healthy environment in countries where life was relatively normal".

It seemed a fantastic proposal. But the outcry which the report caused in Europe and America put an end to red tape and procrastination—particularly after the "Battle of Downing Street", when a swarm of incensed English spinsters broke the windows of the Foreign Office, penetrated into the building and all but lynched Sir Anthony Eden. Similar events in other capitals at last forced the United Nations to act. The action, once started, was on a grandiose scale.

"Operation SKID" ("Save the Kids") was entrusted to the newly founded UNIHOPE. By Christmas 1957, the plan for dispersing the Russian waifs and strays to Australia, New Zealand, Canada and the United States was blueprinted in detail. Three-quarters of the children were to be billeted with foster parents who had volunteered to take them; the remainder in boarding schools, sanatoria, school farms, etc. The air transport fleet of UNIHOPE, which carried food and prefabs for the "Woolworth towns" to Russia, made their return trips loaded with children—the gallant air-crews' nightmare. By the summer of 1958, six months after the start of "Operation SKID", eighty per cent. of the children had been evacuated; the remaining twenty per cent., hardened young criminals of over fifteen, were sent to specially created reformatory schools in Russia. On June 1st, 1959, the last camp was closed down.

But that was not the end of the story. In the famine areas, despairing Russian, Ukrainian, Armenian mothers disguised their children as *Bezprizornye* and sent them out on the roads to be picked up and sent to the lands of plenty—determined to save them from starvation even at the price of never seeing them again. The flood had diminished to a trickle, but even so several thousand children were shipped every month overseas.

These pseudo-orphans became later on the cause of a dramatic turn of events. It was discovered that nearly all parents, before taking the desperate step of parting with their children, had banded them like migrating birds by some identification mark: amulets, neck-chains, even tattooed initials. A year or so later, as conditions gradually improved, they began to flood the authorities with applications for getting their children back. UNIHOPE had to broadcast and advertise several thousand "wanted" lists over

three continents. From early in 1959 onward the children began
to come back.

The return of these formerly starved little wretches, their
changed physical appearance and mental outlook, their manners
and clothes, were a miracle in the eyes of the Russians—and
one of the greatest feats of political propaganda brought about
unintentionally. UNIHOPE was now swamped with pathetic
requests from parents to send their children for a year's health cure
abroad. (One should remember that even to-day the average
ration is under 1,800 calories per head, and that in many areas
these rations exist only on paper.) It was obvious, however, that
UNIHOPE could not go on indefinitely carting children over the
world. That is how the idea of the Lottery was born.

Instead of selecting children for the limited number of available
places by investigating the economic situation of the parents—
which would have been a hopelessly cumbersome procedure
leading to jealousies and complaints—the selection of applicants
was made by lottery. Each town and administrative district had
its small quota, and the lucky ones' names were chosen in public
at the quarterly draws. These draws, followed by the distribution
of consolation prizes in the shape of toys, picture books and huge
quantities of ice-cream, became extremely popular not only
among children but among grown-ups as well. The programme
soon included musical recitals, Punch and Judy shows, and was
wound up by a dance. In every town "Draw Day" became a kind
of popular festival, replacing the traditional Russian fair.

As the Lottery craze grew, the planning committee of
UNIPROD (United Nations Political Re-education Department)
had the inspiration to extend the scheme to adults. Having lived
cut off from the rest of the world for nearly half a century, the one
overwhelming desire of every Russian was to visit the mysterious
countries abroad—if only for a month, a day, or an hour. The
returning children's tales had been the most effective propaganda

for the ways of the free world—each of them worth a million dollars spent on UNIPROD's vapid broadcasts and tons of its tedious pamphlets. Obviously, the most effective method of political re-education was to try the same thing with adults—journalists, doctors, teachers, industrial managers, farmers.

The project now consists in guided three-months tours for 100,000 professional men per year, in those countries where they are able to learn most in their speciality. The "quotas" are apportioned both by geographical regions and professional groups. In this way we may hope to destroy within a few years the last vestiges of the Curtain, and the tenacious psychological after-effects of the past. Although the average citizen's chances of having his name drawn is less than one in a thousand, the national craze is still unabated to-day. The Russians are gamblers at heart, and the "*Lotereya*" appeals more to their imagination than lcetures and arguments.

Already most towns and rural centres have their nucleus of lottery-winners whose eyes have seen our way of life, whose minds have been re-awakened by the shock of contact with a different reality. They have become missionaries of the free world, but in their own manner, their own uniquely Russian way; and it is perhaps not too optimistic to assume that they will gradually succeed to the defunct "Party" in the intellectual leadership of the country.

THE CONVICTS' REPUBLIC

Magadan, Kolyma Peninsula, August 1st

On the road to the settlement at "Kilometer 64", Berzin, Temporary Administrator of the Convicts' Republic of Kolyma, explained:

"There are three basic facts about Kolyma. It is the region

where the lowest temperatures on earth have been recorded. It is the richest gold-mining region in the world. It is a region, six times the size of France, which was for twenty years administered as a single Forced Labour Camp, with ninety per cent. of its population convicts . . ."

He did not speak again for a few miles, when he stopped the car near a group of labourers working on a cabbage-patch. We got out in the sweltering heat—for a hundred days, from June to August, the sun does not set over Kolyma. The workmen, like ourselves, wore mittens and mosquito nets to protect their faces against the swarms of insects which were buzzing around them in a dense cloud. These gnats, midges and gadflies are the scourge of Kolyma in summer, as scurvy, frost-bite and gangrene are in winter.

Berzin borrowed a spade from the workmen and marched our party across the cabbage field. He halted at the edge of the swamp which filled the bleak landscape until it merged into the dark hue of the *taiga*—the virgin forest, stretching for a thousand miles to the Arctic Ocean. He handed me the spade and said: "Try it."

Sweating under the thick net and unable to wipe the sweat from my eyes, I dug into the soft, squashy earth. About ten inches down the spade suddenly struck a hard surface which felt like rock. Berzin smiled with the non-paralysed half of his face. "What do you think it is?"

"I don't know. Gold?"

"No. Ice."

He explained that even during the summer the earth only thaws to a depth of nine or ten inches; underneath, covering the whole Peninsula, lies a stratum of "geological ice", several hundred feet thick.

During the ten weeks of the Polar night the temperature here often drops below minus fifty degrees Fahrenheit. The blizzards reach such a savage fury that even in Magadan, the capital, ropes have to be stretched from house to house to which people can cling when forced to go outdoors—otherwise they would be swept into the sea. In the winter camps, far inside this land of white death, less than half of the slaves used to survive the Polar night. In some of the camps not a single living being was found when the roads opened in spring—convicts, guards and dogs were buried under the same indifferent blanket of snow.

During the first years of colonisation, in the early 1930s, only one in five of the convicts survived eighteen months in Kolyma. Towards the end, the mortality was thirty per cent. per annum. That gave a man an average expected life-span of three years; but the average spans of their sentences were ten, twenty and twenty-five years.

There is a cliché about our times reverting to "dark medieval days". But the Middle Ages had no horrors comparable in extent to the slave-continents of Kolyma, of the Baikal-Amur region, of the Vorkuta and Pechora camps, with their fifteen to twenty million starving, freezing, tattered, vermin-ridden inmates, condemned to slow death after the last inch of labour had been squeezed out of them. Even in antiquity, even among primitive and barbarian civilisations, such an ocean of suffering was never inflicted on such a mass of human lives. Here human evolution had touched the bottom—and until about 1955 it looked as if it would never recover again.

The men and women of Kolyma developed a special mentality. Some had lived in the camps for five, ten or fifteen years; some had been sent to the camps as children, others were born in the camps and had never been past the barbed-wire fence and the machine-gun turrets. This special mentality has to be borne in mind if one tries to understand the developments in Kolyma and in some of the other vast convict districts since the war.

Here, in a nutshell, is what happened in Kolyma.

The Shadow of a Tree

The Peninsula lies at a distance of six thousand miles from the centre of European Russia. In peacetime, the unwilling travellers reached Kolyma by the Trans-Siberian Railway from Moscow to Vladivostok, and continued the journey by boat, past Sakhalin and across the Sea of Okhotsk. Since the war, all land and sea communications had been cut off, and the sparse supplies which reached Kolyma came by air. Even now, three years after the end of the war, with guerilla fights still raging in the Urals and around Lake Baikal, the region can only be approached by a somewhat hazardous air journey. Thus, for the approximately two million deportees on Kolyma, return home has so far been impossible.

I should mention here that for the majority of them the word "home" is an abstraction. The deportee was cut off from communication with his family, which was not even informed of his death. Besides, all members of a deportee's family were themselves automatically liable to deportation to different camps. As a measure of mental self-protection, the convict had to erase all hopes of a happy reunion, and to banish the very word "home" from his mind.

This was particularly true of the Chinese, Mongolian, Tibetan and Korean prisoners who, since the beginning of the Great China Purge in 1951, arrived in growing numbers, until they formed more than fifty per cent. of the slave population.

The slaves of Kolyma were not allowed to read newspapers, but prisoners employed in clerical jobs snatched up bits of information from the radio. After the flight of the Government from Moscow, the collapse of organised resistance could no longer be concealed. It led to mass-desertions among the guards and a break-down of discipline.

The first mutiny occurred at the camp of Elgen on the Taskan River, a hundred and fifty-five miles north-west of Magadan. The slaves got hold of an amount of high explosives used on road-building, blew up the machine-gun towers, overpowered and

167

killed the remaining guards. The heaviest losses were inflicted upon them, not by the demoralised guards, but by the pack of wolfhounds which were a standing feature of every Kolyma camp. That is how Berzin, the leader of the mutiny, had half his face lacerated and permanently paralysed.

From Elgen the insurgents set out in trucks and jeeps, armed with the garrison's weapons, for Yagodnoye, the next big camp, thirty miles away. The guards at Yagodnoye were taken by surprise and surrendered. After a summary trial by the prisoners, all guards, with the exception of two who had a reputation for humanity, were driven into the marshes and shot.

After Yagodnoye, it was the turn of Talon, Balagannoye and finally of the capital, Magadan. Left without authority or directives, and fearful about their own future, the MVD detachments accepted their fate with resignation and only resisted sporadically. The small minority of free citizens in Magadan and the other centres were quick to turn their coats when the wind changed. After the fall of Magadan, the whole huge territory, from the Lena and Aldan Rivers to the Amur and the Pacific Ocean, became an administrative No-Man's Land.

The second and much bloodier phase of the struggle was fought between the nascent Convicts' Republic and the common criminals who represented one-fourth of the population of the camps. In all civilised countries, including Czarist Russia, political prisoners enjoyed preferential treatment over criminals. The totalitarian régimes reversed this procedure. In Nazi and Soviet concentration camps the common criminals were put in charge as barrack elders and foremen of the labour gangs. The *urki*, as the Russian criminals call themselves, had a free hand to rob, brutalise and denounce the political prisoners, and to work them to death in the brigades under their command. The *urki* were worse than the wolfhounds, and hardly more humane.

After the rebellion, an attempt was made to integrate them

into the new community, but it failed. The criminals remained a disruptive element who, through theft, drunkenness, rape and murder, made life intolerable. During the Polar night of 1957, a ghastly civil war was fought all over Kolyma which ended with the eviction of the *urki* from the cities and camps. Most of them perished in the *taiga*; a few went over to the politicals and were accepted; several thousand are said to have made their way to the inaccessible regions of the north where they live by preying on the native hunting and fishing tribes—the Yakuts and Chukchi.

After that, Berzin and his colleagues could start bringing some semblance of order into the vast kingdom which had so unexpectedly fallen into their lap—a kingdom of two million starved convicts who found themselves in temporary possession of the richest gold deposits on our earth.

At the outbreak of the second World War, the Kolyma mines produced four to five million ounces of gold per year, while the total output of the rest of the world was thirty-two million ounces. Between the second and third war, the Kolyma output rose further, while production in the rest of the world declined; so the Convict Republic was in potential control of twenty to thirty per cent. of the world's gold resources.

Nobody had foreseen this turn of events. In the general blueprint for the occupation period, all natural resources, mines and industries were to be administered by the provisional Russian Government under the supervision of UNITOC. But UNITOC's authority still ends roughly at the Urals; in Asiatic Russia it only controls certain key regions, such as Kamchatka, Sakhalin and the towns along the Trans-Siberian Railway. The only way of getting control of Kolyma would have been to land allied troops —a step which was fraught with the danger of international complications. The future of the Kolyma gold was already the subject of jealousies and intrigues among the Allies; besides, a sudden influx of a quarter of the world's gold production would have a disrupting effect on world economy. The God-forsaken Peninsula on its layer of geological ice became one of the worst headaches for the victors.

The solution of the dilemma—and of a number of related problems—came with the founding of UNIHOPE. In retrospect, the decision to use the Kolyma gold for financing UNIHOPE's gigantic rehabilitation enterprise seems only logical; but to have taken this logical step at the time was a considerable feat of imagination and statesmanship—and one of the truly great decisions which shaped the future of mankind.

Once the decision was taken, the problem of administering the Peninsula ceased to be political dynamite, and became a question of technical efficiency. Evidently, the gold could only be mined by the men on the spot. The men had constituted themselves an Autonomous Convicts' Republic, "pending the election by the Constituent National Assembly of an all-Russian central government, and until such time as this elected government is capable of exercising effective control". Their proclamation was in accordance with Point Seven of the United Nations Temporary Occupation Charter, which encouraged the formation of *de facto* local administrations in liberated Asia. In other respects too, the proclamation was reasonable and businesslike. It was mainly the work of Dr. Hsiao, a former Professor of International Law at the University of Peking, who had been sentenced to twenty years for "counter-revolutionary, Trotskyite-Maoist propaganda", and had survived five years of Kolyma as a latrine cleaner.

The main points of the proclamation were that the "Temporary Administration" of the Republic should function under the supervision of UNITOC but enjoy local autonomy under Point Seven of the Charter; that the total amount of gold mined should be surrendered to UNIHOPE in exchange for food, housing, clothing, medical supplies, and the gradual repatriation of those desiring to return to their countries of origin, as soon as conditions permitted.

Three days after the first radio communication had been received by UN headquarters on Sakhalin, the first mission of UNIHOPE landed at the airport of Magadan. It was headed by Brigadier-General Sir Robert Manningham-Ward, D.S.O., C.B.E., who had looked at this mission with some misgivings, and was agreeably surprised by the reception he met. In his first letter to Lady Manningham-Ward, he wrote:

"These convict leaders are not only eminently reasonable, but some of them, like Professor Hsiao, are delightful chaps. What's more, Hsiao has been to Eton and has managed to preserve his tie, but had to use it, I am sorry to say, for foot rags. He says it saved his remaining six toes."

Kolyma, August 5th

Berzin owed his reputation to the fact that he was one of the handful of inmates of Elgen camp really guilty of the charge which led to his conviction. He was convicted at the age of sixteen under Articles 7, 10 and 11 of Paragraph 58 of the Soviet Criminal Code: Sedition; Counter-revolutionary Agitation and Propaganda; and Organisation of Counter-revolutionary Groups. As a schoolboy in Odessa he had participated in the short-lived activity of a group of adolescents whose parents had fallen victims to the purge. The group called itself "Revenge for our Parents" and was promptly rounded up after issuing its first stencilled leaflet. He got fifteen years which, after he had served them, were automatically extended by another ten. The irony of Berzin's story is that his own parents had not been purged; he had joined the organisation for the sake of his girl-friend,

Màsha. After he was caught, his parents, both respected Party members, were of course arrested too; he has never heard of them since. He is now forty-one years old, twenty-five of which were spent in the camp; an unparalleled record of longevity in Kolyma which made him into a legendary figure.

He is short, stocky, has immense physical strength and a mask-like face, half of which is paralysed. He speaks little and listens impassively to others; it is quite impossible to form an idea of the mental world in which he lives—the private universe of a man who for a quarter-century has been a slave, and has yet preserved his dignity and remained a man.

They say he is an "anarchist", though he himself never talks about politics. In this respect Berzin is not an exception. Hardly anyone among the ex-convicts is interested in politics; most of them confess somewhat dubiously that they are "anarchists" and "followers of Tolstoy and Prince Kropotkin". If pressed for an explanation, they will say hesitantly that the source of all evil and the main enemy of man is the State; if the State were abolished all would be well and all men would become brothers. If you try to argue with them, they become confused, and subside into silence. Their notion of "anarchism" is entirely vague, and based on nebulous hearsay. The Chinese majority is illiterate, and the others nearly so. From the moment of their arrest they were deprived of any kind of reading matter—in Berzin's case since the age of sixteen. It is impossible for them to form any clear political idea; politics, like most questions beyond their narrow horizon, make them feel bored and mentally helpless. Their minds, starved of contact with the outside world, have become sluggish; their intellect has atrophied for lack of exercise. Those who have spent more than ten years here are afraid of going back into a world from which they have become estranged. Before their liberation, they worked twelve to fourteen hours a day on starvation rations, under unimaginable conditions of hardship. Now they work six to seven hours, are well-fed, clad, and housed in a manner which seems to them undreamed luxury. But their physical and mental rehabilitation is a slow process, and many are past recovery.

Immediately after the liberation, as food, medicaments and warm clothing began to pour in, the death-rate, for a few weeks, rose steeply. Many convicts who previously had kept a precarious hold on life by sheer power of will, died when the tension in them snapped and their will relaxed. A short while later, a wave of alcoholism swept Kolyma, until Berzin and his colleagues were forced to resort to prohibition. Other fashions and crazes followed. To be constantly hurried by the guards and *urki* had become second nature to the convicts, so that they did not know what to do with the long hours of leisure which were suddenly theirs. Boredom and restlessness, particularly during the months of the Polar night, led to a mania for gambling, knitting and embroidery; the men also took to keeping strange animal pets and to inventing complicated culinary dishes—the longer they took to prepare, the better.

Kolyma, August 6th

One of the curiosities of Kolyma is the immense popularity of the "story-tellers" who, in the absence of books, had become a standing institution in all Soviet prisons and labour camps. The story-teller rarely invented his yarn; mostly he gave his own version of novels and stories which he had read in bygone days. The age of slavery had led to a revival of the bards.

In the camps, the story-teller was the only person whose life and possessions were safe, even from the criminals. In the free Convicts' Republic he has become a highly paid professional. Having lost the reading habit, large numbers of the workers prefer to gather in the evenings in the recreation room and to listen to the bard's condensed, but all the more colourful version of *Anna Karenina, Hamlet* or *The Arabian Nights.*

The main problem, and an unsolved one, which prevents return to full normality, is the absence of women. The proportion of female to male prisoners in the camps was about one to a hundred. Here in Kolyma, the poet's praise of the woman "who is worth her weight in gold" has come unexpectedly true, regardless of the lady's age and appearance. This led to certain developments otherwise only found in primitive societies. One of them is polyandry—several husbands sharing one woman.

Kolyma, August 9th

. . . Four years have passed since the mutiny of Elgen brought liberation to the slaves of Kolyma. Even this sketchy report may convey an idea of the deep injuries which the bodies and souls of these men have suffered, of the slowness of the process of recovery, and the great number of those in whom the human substance has deteriorated beyond repair.

All tyrannies carry the seed of their own destruction—but at what price, at what terrible price for humanity.

Kolyma, August 10th

Hsiao gave a small party in his house; Berzin was there, and two other members of the Temporary Administration. One was a tall, fidgety man, a former school-teacher from Latvia, who is in charge of the public re-education programme; he made a somewhat dispirited impression. The other was Mother Seraphimova, an old Russian peasant-woman with a wrinkled face and young eyes, who hardly said a word during the whole evening and probably understood little of what was said, but whose presence radiated a strange feeling of peace. Seraphimova is illiterate and has no particular function in the Government; but she was unanimously elected because of this indefinable quality which seems to have a purifying effect on everybody who comes in contact with her. She is perhaps as nearly a saint as people can be at this time and in this place. I ought to mention that every slave camp had its "saint", just as it had its story-teller.

We drank tea and talked; the conversation was rather halting. Towards the end of the evening I asked Hsiao what lesson Kolyma had taught him. He smiled embarrassedly; it was then that Seraphimova spoke for the first time. She said:

"Show him your pictures."

Hsiao rose and came back after a little while with some ink drawings he had made. They were landscapes in the classic Chinese tradition: a few of the sad, sparse larch trees of Kolyma; tattered men being marched to work; in the background the monotonous skyline of the *taiga*, and the desolate cliffs which close in the harbour of Magadan.

"They are quite unworthy," said Hsiao, actually blushing. "But this is what Kolyma taught me."

He pointed a thin, yellow finger at the figures in the foreground; and then I saw what he meant. The men and the trees in the landscape had shadows. From time immemorial, Chinese painters had made their pictures without shadows in them.

"You see," he explained, "for three months in summer the sun never sets in Kolyma. The light is almost horizontal; so a tree, throws a very long shadow. One day I suddenly *saw* the shadow of a tree and I discovered that my picture would not be complete without it; so I put it in. For a painter grown up in the classic Chinese tradition, this was a very daring thing to do. All real revolutions happen in the minds of people. They will happen as long as there are men—even in Kolyma. Everything else is of little importance."

Moscow, August 15th

Back from Kolyma.

I must have caught some kind of fever in the gnat-infested swamps, for last night I was plagued by a nightmare. I dreamt that UNIHOPE, and the free Convict Republic, and the rescue of the children, and the Great Lottery, only existed in my own imagination—a dream born out of frustration and despair; and that in reality vengefulness, rapacious greed and blindness of heart have made the victors repeat the blunders of the past, and throw away humanity's last chance of salvation. I woke up, drenched in cold sweat, among the crawling bugs.

III

THE FAILURE OF
RESPONSE

The Right To Say "No"

FOUR CONTRIBUTIONS TO THE CONGRESS
FOR CULTURAL FREEDOM

The Congress for Cultural Freedom, an international meeting of writers, scholars and scientists under the patronage of Bertrand Russell, Benedetto Croce, John Dewey, Karl Jaspers, and Jacques Maritain, was held in June, 1950 in Berlin. Its opening session coincided with the beginning of the Korean war. It served a double purpose: as a kind of intellectual airlift, a demonstration of Western solidarity with the brave and battered outpost of Berlin, a hundred miles behind the Iron Curtain; and as an attempt to dispel the intellectual confusion created by the totalitarian campaigns under the slogan of peace. Out of the deliberations of the Berlin Congress arose an international movement with branches and publications in a number of European, American and Asiatic countries, among them Encounter, *London, and* Preuves, *Paris.*

I. MANIFESTO OF THE CONGRESS FOR
CULTURAL FREEDOM★

1. We hold it to be self-evident that intellectual freedom is one of the inalienable rights of man.

★ The manifesto, drafted by request of the steering committee, was unanimously adopted at the closing session of the Congress on 30th June, 1950. The words in square brackets were added to my draft by the British members of the editorial committee, Professor A. J. Ayer and Mr. Trevor-Roper.

2. Such freedom is defined first and foremost by his right to hold and express his own opinions, and particularly opinions which differ from those of his rulers. Deprived of the right to say "no", man becomes a slave.

3. Freedom and peace are inseparable. In any country, under any régime, the overwhelming majority of ordinary people fear and oppose war. The danger of war becomes acute when governments, by suppressing democratic representative institutions, deny to the majority the means of imposing its will to peace.

Peace can be maintained only if each government submits to the control and inspection of its acts by the people whom it governs, and agrees to submit all questions immediately involving the risk of war to a representative international authority, by whose decision it will abide.

4. We hold that the main reason for the present insecurity of the world is the policy of governments which, while paying lip-service to peace, refuse to accept this double control. Historical experience proves that wars can be prepared and waged under any slogan, including that of peace. Campaigns for peace which are not backed by acts that will guarantee its maintenance are like counterfeit currency circulated for dishonest purposes. Intellectual sanity and physical security can only return to the world if such practices are abandoned.

5. Freedom is based on the toleration of divergent opinions. The principle of toleration does not logically permit the practice of intolerance.

6. No political philosophy or economic theory can claim the sole right to represent freedom in the abstract. We hold that the value of such theories is to be judged by the range of concrete freedom which they accord the individual in practice.

We likewise hold that no race, nation, class or religion can claim the sole right to represent the idea of freedom, nor the right to deny freedom to other groups or creeds in the name of any ultimate ideal or lofty aim whatsover. We hold that the historical contribution of any society is to be judged by the extent and quality of the freedom which its members actually enjoy.

7. In times of emergency, restrictions on the freedom of the individual are imposed in the real or assumed interest of the community. We hold it to be essential that such restrictions be confined to a minimum of clearly specified actions; that they be understood to be temporary and limited expedients in the nature of a sacrifice; and that the measures restricting freedom be themselves subject to free criticism and democratic control. Only thus can we have a reasonable assurance that emergency measures restricting individual freedom will not degenerate into a permanent tyranny.

8. In totalitarian states restrictions on freedom are no longer intended and publicly understood as a sacrifice imposed on the people, but are on the contrary represented as triumphs of progress and achievements of a superior civilisation. We hold that both the theory and practice of these régimes run counter to the basic rights of the individual and the fundamental aspirations of mankind as a whole.

9. We hold the danger represented by these régimes to be all the greater since their means of enforcement far surpasses that of all previous tyrannies in the history of mankind. The citizen of the totalitarian state is expected and forced not only to abstain from crime but to conform in all his thoughts and actions to a prescribed pattern. Citizens are persecuted and condemned on such unspecified and all-embracing charges as "enemies of the people" or "socially unreliable elements".

10. We hold that there can be no stable world so long as mankind, with regard to freedom, remains divided into "haves" and "have-nots". The defence of existing freedoms, the reconquest of lost freedoms [and the creation of new freedoms], are parts of the same struggle.

11. We hold that the theory and practice of the totalitarian state are the greatest challenge which man has been called on to meet in the course of civilised history.

12. We hold that indifference or neutrality in the face of such a challenge amounts to a betrayal of mankind and to the abdication of the free mind. Our answer to this challenge may decide the fate of man for generations.

13. [The defence of intellectual liberty to-day imposes a positive obligation: to offer new and constructive answers to the probems of our time.]

14. We address this manifesto to all men who are determined to regain those liberties which they have lost, and to preserve [and extend] those which they enjoy.

The Right to Say "No"

II. TWO METHODS OF ACTION

Address delivered (in German) at the opening session of the Congress for Cultural Freedom, 25th June, 1950

Since the earliest days, the teachers of mankind have recommended two diametrically opposed methods of action. The first demands that we should refuse to see the world divided into black and white, heroes and villains, friends and foes; that we should distinguish nuances, and strive for synthesis or at least compromise; it tells us that in nearly all, seemingly inescapable dilemmas there exists a third alternative which patient search may discover. In short, we should refuse the choice between Scylla and Charybdis and rather navigate like Odysseus of the nimble wits. We may call this the "neither-nor" attitude.

The second, opposite advice was summed up two thousand years ago in one single phrase: "Let your communication be, Yea, yea, Nay, nay; for whatsoever is more than these, comes from evil." This we may call the "either-or" attitude.

Obviously humanity could not have survived without taking both methods into account. By neglecting the first advice, men would long ago have torn each other to pieces. By neglecting the second, man would have forsaken his dignity and moral backbone, and lost his capacity to distinguish between good and evil.

It is equally obvious that each of the two tenets has a different field of application. To enumerate these would be a tedious and pedantic undertaking, and frequently there is conflict between both methods within the same field. Our concern here is with action in the political field. And there it seems that the first method is valid for long-term planning with a certain elbow-room in space and time, and that the second is valid in immediate and vital emergencies when, in Beethoven's words, "Fate knocks at the gate of existence".

In such an emergency, the threatened individual or group or civilisation can only survive if it acts with the unhesitating assurance of an organic reflex. The nerves of all living organisms function according to the so-called all-or-nothing law; they either react to a stimulus for all they are worth or do not react at all. And it is not by chance that the calculating machines called electronic brains are constructed according to the same "either-or" principle. They perform immensely complex functions, but each time a decision is required of them, they act according to the Gospel of Matthew.

In vital emergencies like the present, when man stands at a crossroads which only leaves the choice of this way or that, the difference between the very clever and the simple in mind narrows almost to vanishing point, or even turns to the latter's advantage. It is amazing to observe how in a crisis the most sophisticated often act like imbeciles. Imbued with the mental habits of the "neither-nor" attitude, of looking for synthesis or compromise—a profoundly human attitude of essential value in its proper field—they are incapable of admitting, even to themselves, that there are situations in which an unambiguous decision is vital for spiritual and physical survival. Faced with destiny's challenge, they act like clever imbeciles and preach neutrality towards the bubonic plague. Mostly they are victims of a professional disease: the intellectual's estrangement from reality. And having lost touch with reality they have acquired that devilish art: they can prove everything that they believe, and believe everything that they can prove. Their logic reminds one of the German students' old nonsense-song:

The elephant has his tail in front and his trunk is at his rear;
But when he turns round his trunk is in front and his tail is at his rear.

184

The Right to Say "No"

Don't misunderstand me: I know that many of those who are not here with us to-day cherish freedom too, and are rather frightened of the fate which might befall them if everybody imitated their attitude of contemplative detachment. It is only that they haven't yet learnt that there is a time to speak in relative clauses, and a time to speak in terms of Yea and Nay. For destiny's challenge to man is always couched in simple and direct language, without relative clauses—and requires an answer in equally simple terms.

III. AN OUTGROWN DILEMMA

Revised version of a talk to the political panel session of the
congress for Cultural Freedom, June, 1950

The thesis which I wish to put before you is that the antimonies
"Socialism and Capitalism", "Left and Right", are rapidly becoming meaningless, and that so long as Europe remains bogged
down in these false alternatives which obstruct clear thinking, it
cannot hope to find a constructive solution for its problems.

1

The term "Political Left" originated, as you know, with the
distribution of factions in the French National Assembly after
the Revolution in 1789. At the beginning of the nineteenth
century it spread over the Continent and was applied to that
section of a country's legislature which sat to the left of the
President's chair and was traditionally associated with liberal and
democratic opinions. Gradually, the word came to mean the
radical or purist or extremist wing of any ideological school or
movement, whether liberal and democratic or not. Later on it was
used in an even more vague and metaphorical way; and the more
it was drained of meaning, the stronger became its emotional
appeal. At the beginning of the last war there existed about half
a dozen political parties in France, all of them conservative to
reactionary in their programme, all of them seated in the right
wing of the Chamber, and all of them carrying the word "Left"
in their names.

I mention this development as a semantic curiosity and because
of its relevance to the present situation. For to this day European

The Right to Say "No"

Liberals and Social-Democrats refer to themselves as "the moderate Left" which, if words are to be taken seriously, must mean that they differ only in degree but not in kind from their neighbours of "the extreme Left." And "the extreme Left" is still regarded as synonymous with the Communist Party, in spite of the fact that virtually every tenet in the Communist *credo* is diametrically opposed to the principles originally associated with the Left. In short, the term "Left" has become a verbal fetish whose cult sidetracks attention from the real issues. It is at the same time a dangerous anachronism, for it implies the existence of a continuous spectrum between liberal progressives and the worshippers of tyranny and terror. And such is the magic power of words over the mind that European Socialists who think of themselves as "men of the Left" were unconsciously led from a fallacious verbal identification to a real feeling of solidarity with the Communists. They may feel critical or even hostile towards their "extreme" neighbours of the Communist Party; they retain nevertheless an ambivalent neighbourly feeling for them, a conviction of "having the same historical roots," of being, after all, "on the same side of the barricades".

A good many American liberals fell into the same emotional trap during the 'thirties and even later. The victim of the witch-hunt supplied the whip which scourged him and became an accomplice in his own perdition. However, the relative safety and prosperity of that continent made the confused American liberal gradually accessible to reality and enabled him to get out of the trap, while a major portion of the French and Italian Left, and a smaller portion of the British, exposed to the neurosis-forming climate of Europe, have remained in it.

In the past it was always "the Left" who protested loudest against tyranny, injustice, and infringements of human rights. The failure of European "Leftists" and American liberals to lead the fight against the worst régime of terror and despotism in human history created a strategic vacuum on the ideological battlefield. This vacuum was filled by the Christian Democrats in Italy, the Gaullists in France, by Senator McCarthy and his associates in the U.S.A. McCarthyism represents the wages of the American liberals' sins. If to-day everywhere in the world the parties who claim to represent the "moderate Left" are beaten or in retreat, it is because they were found wanting in the most crucial issue of our time.

2

Europe has developed a political climate under which words are no longer taken seriously. The ideological chaos created a semantic inflation and a semantic black market where words are traded at a meaning-value entirely different from their official quotation: where war is prepared by peace petitions, police states are labelled popular democracies, and "Leftism" means benevolent neutrality towards despotism.

At first sight the alternative "Capitalism or Socialism" appears much more concrete and meaningful than "Right or Left". But on closer inspection it will be found that the term "Socialism" has suffered a semantic decay similar to that of the "Left". German National Socialism, Russian Soviet Socialism; French Socialism which is Marxist with a pinch of salt, British Socialism which is Christian, non-Marxist, Fabianist, and heaven knows what, all derive their emotional dynamism from the fetish-power of the same word, attached to quite different meanings.

However, let us leave semantics aside, though it is an essential branch of political hygiene. If we are not too pedantic, we may hope to agree at least on some rough-and-ready definition of what Socialism really means, and on some common denominator for the aspirations of the various existing Socialist parties.

Let us turn first to the field of *international* politics. One of the basic elements of Socialist thought, from Spartacus's slave revolt to Thomas More's *Utopia*, from the primitive Christian communities to Marx, is the brotherhood of man. In the past, Socialists have always fought against parochialism, chauvinism, aggressive nationalism and have preached internationalism, cosmopolitanism, the abolition of ideological and political barriers among nations. But do they still?

In the Union of Soviet Socialist Republics the word "cosmopolitan" has become a term of abuse, and chauvinism has reached a hitherto unprecedented peak. At the same time at the recent Paris Congress of the French Communist Party a banner was stretched across the hall which read: "The true internationalist is he who is prepared unreservedly, unhesitatingly, and unconditionally to defend the U.S.S.R." So much for the Russian version of Socialist internationalism.

In the Western world the only great power with a Socialist Government is Great Britain. The Labour Party won the elections a few weeks after the end of the war in the still strongest country of Europe, and just at the decisive moment when it no longer needed a Socialist training to understand that Europe must unite or perish. Never before in history was Socialism offered such a chance. Yet from the moment it came to power, the Labour Government has deliberately obstructed every effort towards European unity. The non-Socialist Governments of France, Germany and Italy have proved themselves more internationally-minded than the Socialist Government in England.

Of course Britain has a particularly difficult position between the Continent and the Commonwealth; and there are always plausible arguments for avoiding decisions which would require a certain amount of historical imagination. But the essential point is that the victory of British Socialism has not abolished British insularity; it has, on the contrary, strengthened and deepened it. It was Churchill the Conservative, not Attlee the Socialist, who started the United Europe movement which led to the Council of Strasbourg; and when the movement got under way, the Labour Party's attitude to it remained consistently hostile. The reason for this was explained in a statement by the National Executive Committee of the Labour Party issued in June, 1950. "No Socialist government in Europe," the decisive phrase in the statement runs, "could submit to the authority of a [supranational] body whose policies were decided by an anti-Socialist majority."

What this amounts to is simply a mild British version of the Russian "Socialism in One Country" policy. The Russian veto in the United Nations finds its equivalent in the British veto against the political and economic unity of Europe.

It need not be emphasised that there is a world of difference between the British and the Soviet régimes. My comparison refers merely to one specific aspect; the collapse of the cosmopolitan *élan* in the Socialist movement. This process started almost a generation ago, in 1914, and has now reached a stage where we can see the paradoxical phenomenon of capitalist America being prepared to make sacrifices in national sovereignty which Socialist Russia refuses, and of British, French, and German Conservatives pursuing a more internationally-minded policy than their Socialist opposite numbers. In other words, *Socialism has lost its claim to represent the internationalist trend of humanity*. As far as the integration of our world is concerned, the Socialist-Capitalist alternative has become void of meaning.

Is it more meaningful when applied to *domestic* policy?

As regards political and intellectual freedom, there is no relevant difference between Socialist Britain and the capitalist United States. And in the domain of unfreedom there is little to choose between Socialist Russia and Fascist Spain. Again the real division cuts across the abstract frontiers between Socialism and Capitalism. Only one field remains where the alternative is apparently still relevant: the economic field.

The Right to Say "No"

Theoretically there is an unbridgeable gulf between nationalisation of the means of production on the one hand, and private ownership, profits, and exploitation on the other. But in fact recent developments have abolished the static trench-warfare between the classes and have transformed it into a fluid war of movement. As the question is too complex to be treated here in any systematic manner, I must confine myself to a few remarks in shorthand, as it were.

First, even Marx and Engels knew that nationalisation itself is not a panacea. It is useful to recall Frederick Engels' remark that if nationalisation were identical with Socialism, then the first Socialist institution must have been the regimental tailor. In fact, the Soviet workers do not own their nationalised factories any more than a sailor of the Royal Navy owns the battleship in which he serves. The people's control over the battleships, railways, factories, coal mines, which they theoretically own, depends entirely on the political structure of the state. In Russia, where the Trade Unions have ceased to be an instrument of the working class and have become an instrument for the coercion of the working class, the theoretical owners of the factories and of the land have less influence over management, and work under worse conditions, than their comrades in any Western country. On the other hand, trust managers, factory directors, and "proletarian millionaires" (an official Russian term) form a privileged class, just as much as and more so, than in capitalist countries. To be sure, their income is called salary and not profit, but again this distinction is mainly abstract. Nor is, on the other hand, the factory owner in capitalist countries any longer able to draw unlimited profits from his enterprise or do with his workers what he likes. I refer you to James Burnham's analysis of the relevant changes in the meaning of the term "ownership" in recent times.

Generally speaking, nationalisation without an appropriate

change in political structure leads not to State Socialism but to State Capitalism. The difference between the two cannot be defined in economic terms; it is a matter of democratic controls, of political freedom, and cultural climate. A nationalised economy in itself may serve as a basis for a totalitarian autocracy of the Russian type or even for a Fascist régime.

Equally problematic is the question just *how much* nationalisation makes a country socialist or capitalist? British Socialism nationalised the railways, but France and Germany had state-owned railways long before. The total nationalisation of all means of production and distribution has been recognised as unworkable even in Russia. The alternative is no longer national-isation or private economy in the abstract; the real problem is to find the proper balance of state ownership, control, planning, and free enterprise. And the search for this delicate balance is again not an abstract but an empirical pursuit. Apparently each nation has to work out its own formula, for there are many impondera-bilia which enter into the equation.

As an example of the complex reality masked by the "Capital-ism versus Socialism" slogan, one may quote food-rationing. Food-rationing—which means state control of distribution—worked very satisfactorily in puritan England under Conservative and Socialist governments alike. But it broke down completely in Italy and France, both countries with a highly individualistic and resourceful Latin population. Obviously, far-reaching infer-ences must be drawn from this fact concerning the balance of state control and free enterprise appropriate to each of these countries. In short, even in the purely economic sphere we are not dealing with a clear-cut alternative between Capitalism and Socialism, but with a kind of continuous rainbow spectrum whose shape and colour are largely determined by psychological and other factors not contained in Socialist theory.

3

What I have said should not be misinterpreted as an apology for Capitalism or as an attack on Socialism. My point is that this alternative is rapidly becoming as antiquated and meaningless as the dispute between Jansenists and Jesuits or the Wars of the Roses. Nor did I mean to say that it always *was* meaningless. I said it is *becoming* meaningless, because it operates with rigid nineteenth-century conceptions, and does not take into account new realities which have emerged since, and new conflicts which cut across the conventional boundaries.

It is not a novelty in history that a real dilemma which once seemed all-important is gradually drained of its meaning and becomes a pseudo-dilemma as new historical realities emerge. People lost interest in waging wars of religion when national consciousness began to dawn on them. The conflict between republicans and monarchists went out of fashion when economic problems became all-important. The examples could be multiplied. Every period seems to have its specific conflict which polarises the world and serves as an ideological compass in the chaos —until history passes over it with a shrug; and afterwards people wonder what they were so excited about.

It is a further fact that some of these great ideological conflicts are never decided; they end in a stalemate. In successive centuries it looked as if the whole world would either become Islamic or Christian, either Catholic or Protestant, either republican or monarchist, either capitalist or socialist. But instead of a decision there came a deadlock and a process which one might call *the withering away of the dilemma*. The withering, or draining of meaning, always seems to be the result of some mutation in human consciousness accompanied by a shift of emphasis to

an entirely different set of values—from religious consciousness to national consciousness to economic consciousness and
so on.

This "and so on" poses a problem which we are unable to
answer with certainty. We cannot foretell the nature of the next
mutation in the consciousness of the masses, nor the values which
will emerge on the next higher level. But we may assume on the
strength of past analogies that the battle-cries of economic man
will appear to his successor just as sterile and pointless as the Wars
of the Roses appear to us.

Two short remarks in conclusion. First, it is necessary to
qualify the statement that the apparently decisive conflicts of a
given period tend to end in a stalemate and wither away. This
did indeed happen in the past, but only in cases where the forces
in the conflict were fairly balanced. Europe remained Christian
because the Arabs never got to Paris and the Turks were beaten
back at the ramparts of Vienna. There are other, less edifying
examples of history solving its dilemmas. The conclusion is
obvious.

In the second place, though we cannot foresee the values and
spiritual climate of post-economic man, certain conjectures are
permissible. While the majority of Europeans are still hypnotised by the anachronistic battle-cries of Left and Right, Capitalism
and Socialism, history has moved on to a new alternative, a new
conflict which cuts across the old lines of division. The real content of this conflict can be summed up in one phrase: total
tyranny against relative freedom. Sometimes I have a feeling in
my bones that the terrible pressure which this conflict exerts on
all humanity might perhaps represent a challenge, a biological
stimulus as it were, which will release the new mutation of
human consciousness; and that its content might be a new
spiritual awareness, born of anguish and suffering, of the full

meaning of freedom. And I don't mean by that, freedom from want, freedom from fear and the rest. Since the dawn of civilisation people have fought under the slogan of freedom; but it was always freedom *from* some particularly irksome oppression, freedom in a restricted, negative sense. I mean freedom in a much deeper and fuller sense than any we can conceive to-day, or see realised anywhere in organic nature. If that is the case, then we are indeed living in an interesting time, and the answer which we shall give to destiny's challenge is not without import for the future of our species.

IV. QUESTIONS AND ANSWERS

*Abridged text of a pamphlet written anonymously, and originally pub-
lished in French under the title 'Que veulent les Amis de la Liberté?'
by the French Committee for Cultural Freedom, Paris, 1950*

First and foremost, we want our civilisation to survive. Two
conditions are essential for its survival: freedom and peace.

We have put freedom first because peace is a function of
freedom. A nation enslaved can at any time be whipped by its
leaders into war hysteria and aggression. By isolating countries
behind an Iron Curtain or a Chinese Wall, totalitarian governments can preach pacifism to foreign peoples, and world conquest
to their own.

*Nations wax the more aggressive and bellicose, the more they are
deprived of freedom.* The threat to peace came successively from
countries in various degrees of enslavement: militarist Prussia,
Fascist Italy, Nazi Germany, Japan, Soviet Russia. Each of these
countries has made during the present century successive bids for
world conquest in the name of some ideology or secular religion.
Each promised some form of Thousand-Year Reich or social
paradise as a distant aim. Each time, the professed aim served as a
cloak for wars of conquest. Each time, millions of people were
led to their destruction in the name of a phantom.

Communism in its present form has become a phantom
ideology. It has as little to do with Socialism as the medieval
Inquisition and the reign of the Borgias had with the teachings of
Christ. Our civilisation can only be saved if the hypnotic power
of this phantom is broken. This is not a task which any political
party or group can achieve alone. It is an operation of mental
hygiene which can be accomplished only by a joint effort of the

educated classes—of the men in public life, in the arts and letters, in the universities and elementary schools, in the laboratories and editorial offices, in the trade unions and professional organisations—who determine the intellectual climate of the nation.

The task which the Congress for Cultural Freedom and the *Amis de la Liberté* have set for themselves is to change the present confused and poisoned intellectual climate. If we fail, we shall become guilty of a new *trahison des clercs*, and the responsibility before history will be ours.

Since the Berlin Congress launched its Manifesto, its Secretariat has received a flood of letters asking us to clarify our attitude to a number of questions. The following are our answers to some of the questions which seem to us most typical.

Question: How can we pretend to defend freedom while the Western world is rife with social injustice, political corruption, racial discrimination?

Answer: We do not pretend that our democracies are anywhere approaching an ideal state. We are defending our relative freedoms against the total unfreedom of dictatorial régimes.

This is not an abstract distinction. Its validity is demonstrated by the mass exodus of persecuted people from the satellite countries to the West. Europe has become a one-way street which points from total slavery to relative freedom. The wretched masses who have left their homes, their goods and chattels, with no better immediate prospects than physical safety in a D.P. camp, have a bitter knowledge of the reality of our time—a knowledge which a considerable proportion of our intelligentsia lacks.

Question: Does not your militant, anti-totalitarian attitude contribute to making the cold war more acute, and drive us nearer to the hot war?

The Failure of Response

Answer: We are convinced that a militant anti-totalitarian attitude is our last and only chance of preventing war.

Every political and ideological Munich brings war one step nearer.

Every proof that the free world is strong and united makes the danger of war recede one step further.

Every *bona fide* Communist voter brought back into the democratic camp means the loss of one potential Fifth Columnist to the aggressor.

Every fellow-traveller cured of his morbid obsession means one potential collaborator less.

The above goes for the rank and file. Tolerance of mental aberrations cannot be extended to members of the professional intelligentsia. Farm-hands and factory workers labour under the handicap of a fragmentary education, and often it is physically impossible for them to get at the facts. The professional intelligentsia has no such excuses. Refusal to acknowledge facts, conscious or unconscious distortion of facts, frivolity and foolishness on the part of those who influence public opinion, are crimes against the spirit, even if rarely definable by law.

Before the last war, intellectuals who supported Hitler's policy of concentration camps, or refused to admit that German concentration camps existed, were ostracised by progressive intellectuals. The writers and scientists who to-day support Russian concentration camps and mass deportations, or refuse to admit the facts concerning them, are still regarded as "progressive" and "idealistic". We are opposed to the persecution of the ignorant and the innocent. We are opposed to the toleration of the totalitarian creed in the professional intelligentsia. We refuse to grant intellectual respectability to the active or passive accomplices of tyranny, terror and defamation.

Question: Is it possible for a Socialist or a member of the moderate

The Right to Say "No"

Left to co-operate with right-wing political parties against the extreme Left?

Answer: The question contains a semantic fallacy. The parties directed by the Cominform do not represent the "Left". The fact that misguided portions of the working class, for instance in France and Italy, support the Communist party, does not make it a left-wing party. Millions of Italian and German workers enlisted in the Fascist and Nazi parties in an equally mistaken belief, but that did not make Fascism a left-wing movement.

Question: Granted the previous point, I am still not sure whether a real collaboration between Socialists and right-wing parties is possible or even desirable.

Answer: We believe such a collaboration to be both possible and desirable—with certain reservations.

That is is *possible* was proved by our Berlin Congress, where English Labourites and Conservatives, French Socialists and de Gaullists, spoke from the same platform, collaborated in committees and achieved, after long and hard discussion, complete unanimity on the text of our Manifesto, on our future programme, and on the composition of our International Committee and working Secretariat.

This collaboration is *desirable* if its objectives are limited to the task of uniting a free nation against threats to its freedom from within and without, and thus acting as a deterrent against aggression. It is *undesirable* if the slogan of unity serves as a cloak for attempts to suppress the democratic rivalry between political parties and groups.

In other words, an essential distinction must be made between short-term and long-term aims. By long-term aims, we mean the age-old struggle for reform, for social justice, for a more equitable form of government. By short-term aims, we mean the necessity of fighting an immediate emergency.

The Failure of Response

A nation is doomed to perish if a considerable part of its population refuses to fight against an immediate threat unless and until an ideal state of social justice is reached.

A nation is doomed to lose its freedom if its population becomes so frightened by the short-term struggle that all the aims of the long-term struggle are sacrificed.

France collapsed under Hitlerite aggression because it failed to make this clear distinction between long-term and short-term aims, because social and party divisions took priority over the tasks imposed by the immediate emergency.

Europe will share the fate of France in 1939 if it is unable to learn the lessons of the past.

Question: What about Spain?

Answer: We consider Franco's totalitarian régime to be as abhorrent as any other tyranny. But it is unlikely that twenty-five million Spaniards will start a war of aggression against the world, and only too likely that the Soviet régime and its satellites will continue the chain of aggressions they started in Korea. Therefore our emphasis is on the immediate and principal danger from the East, and we refuse to fall into the trap of Cominform propagandists who want to divert our attention and energies from the real threat into a crusade against Francisco Franco.

Question: Your Manifesto protests against totalitarian slavery but is silent on matters like racial discrimination against the Negroes in the United States. Why?

Answer: The answer is much the same as on the Spanish question. Communist propaganda deliberately plays up the Negro question to divert attention from the totalitarian threat and to spread confusion in the progressive camp.

The Cominform propagandists and their intellectual dupes pretend that Negroes are tarred and feathered on every street corner in America.* Accordingly, every small racial disturbance in America is played up in big headlines by the so-called progressive press; whereas the deportation of the population of entire Soviet republics—e.g. the Volga-Germans, the Crimean and Chechen Republics—even if officially admitted, is passed over in silence.

During the ninety years since the abolition of slavery, the condition of Negroes in the United States has steadily, though admittedly much too slowly, improved. This improvement might be compared to a continuously ascending curve; whereas the curve of progress in Russia and its satellite countries shows a sudden break and steep fall into the abyss. To accelerate this improvement, and to obtain complete economic and social equality for Negroes, is part of the struggle for long-term aims which must continue. But it is madness to refuse to fight the danger of the total enslavement of Europe because in the Southern States of America Negroes still have to travel in separate railway compartments. Precisely this madness is echoed every day by highbrow French intellectuals and their cliques.

Question: Communism may be a phantom creed—it nevertheless has a strong emotional dynamism, the power of a secular religion. What creed or mystique can you offer which would counteract this force with equal power?

Answer: None. Don't let us have any illusions on this point. We must face our predicament with realism and honesty.

Fanatical mass movements are always at a temporary advantage against the defenders of civilisation. The invading hordes, whether Mongol, Tartar, Fascist, Nazi or Communist, have the advantage

---

* Incidentally, during the last decade the number of Negroes lynched in the United States has never exceeded two a year. However horrifying even two such crimes are, they only represent a fraction of one per mil of the number of crimes against humanity committed annually by the totalitarian régimes.

of a simple monolithic creed over a complex and divided culture. Neither Capitalist America, nor Socialist Britain, nor Christian-Democrat Italy has been capable of producing a faith with the same dynamism as the Communist phantom-creed. Ours is a defensive battle, as most battles which have saved the continuity of civilisation have been. The difficulty which results from this position is that the freedom which we are defending is taken for granted and not much appreciated by the masses—until they are deprived of it. *Habeas corpus*, civil rights, freedom of expression—nay, such elementary privileges as freedom to change one's job if one so desires, to read two newspapers which express opposite opinions, and to travel freely in one's own country—all these do not add up to a militant creed. To quote Matteotti, freedom is like the air you breathe; you only become conscious of it when the rope is round your neck.

We have no panacea to offer to the manifold problems which beset the civilisation we are defending. We do not wish to embark on a crusade. We have learned the tragic lesson of our times; we are conscious of the fact that most crusades in history have ended in disaster and brought only misery and disillusionment in their wake.

Democracy, by its very nature, can create no conspiratorial instrument comparable to the Cominform, nor produce a counter-phantom to the Communist creed. The weapons in our fight can only be truth, sincerity, courage; an acute sense of reality, and our appreciation of the basic values of our complex civilisation.

To the totalitarian threat and its fanatical creed we oppose an absolute and unconditional No. But our Yes to the civilisation which we are defending leaves full scope for nuances, divergent opinions, social theories and experiment.

We repeat: our aim is survival; and the conditions of survival are freedom and peace. Both are threatened from without

and from within. Defence against foreign and internal aggression is impossible in a poisoned moral atmosphere.

To counteract this poison is the task of the professional and intellectual classes and their responsibility. Only a profound and rapid change of the intellectual climate can deter aggression, and make effective defence possible if aggression occurs. Without the return of moral and intellectual sanity, no economic or military aid can save us. To bring about this return to sanity is the aim of the Congress for Cultural Freedom.

We count on your support.

The European Legion*

1

WESTERN EUROPE is a patient in an iron lung. American economic
and military aid provide it with oxygen, but it cannot live and
breathe by itself. The sickness which paralyses it is not of an
economic nature. Nor is it social strife; nor the Communist
phantom creed. These are symptoms of the disease, but not its
cause. The cause is both deeper and simpler: Europe has lost faith
in itself.

In all serious discussions with Frenchmen, Italians, or Western
Germans, there arrives a moment of truth when this fact is
admitted. The manner of admission may be cynical, or bitter, or
resigned. The explanations and excuses vary according to case.
Some will say that Europe is bled out by its wars; others, that
its will to survive has been sapped by the Communist cancer;
still others will put the blame on the capitalist system, the decline
of Christian faith, on British insularity or "the agents of Wall
Street". Only on one point do all divergent views agree: that in
its present condition, Europe cannot survive.

In the larger part of Europe that civilisation which made its
greatness has already been destroyed, and human life degraded to
the routine of the penitentiary. The remaining, truncated part
is equally doomed—unless there is a radical change in its political
and moral climate. This change, or spiritual revival, is the only

* First published in *The New York Times*, 8th October, 1950.

product which America cannot provide for it. It must come out of Europe itself. In what form? And what policy must America pursue, apart from continuing material assistance, to create the favourable conditions for a European resurrection?

2

Before we can hope to find the right answer to this question, certain wrong answers must be eliminated. These fall mainly into two types of popular fallacies. The first is generally voiced by well-meaning progressives on both sides of the Atlantic. It says, roughly, that the best and only means of resisting Communist expansion, both military and ideological, is through social progress in one's own country. Give land to the landless Italian peasants, higher wages to the French workers, abolish poverty, create prosperity and social justice—and Europe will automatically recover its will to live.

It is a beautiful dream, yet a dream, for it confuses the desirable with the possible. The fight for social reform and economic progress is vitally necessary for the peoples of Europe. But it is not sufficient to ensure their survival against Russian aggression, and it is not sufficient to bring forth, in the measurable future, that moral resurgence which alone can save them.

For one thing, the fight for social and economic justice has been going on for some two or three thousand years, and it is unlikely that the golden age will arrive just in time to stop the next Russian move against Berlin or Yugoslavia. Secondly, as long as Communist-controlled trade unions in France and Italy deliberately sabotage the economic recovery of their own countries, any quick, spectacular improvement in the living standards of the people is ruled out. Finally, social progress may enter into a mis-shapen alliance with national egotism. The British people under Labour rule made substantial gains in social security, old age pensions, national health services and so on; but these gains have been nullified on the European balance sheet by the Labour Party's refusal to accept "any supra-national authority dominated by non-Socialist governments".

Let us repeat, then: the struggle for social progress is necessary, but not sufficient to save Europe; just as vitamin tablets are healthy, but not sufficient to save a patient from a mortal disease.

The second wrong answer is related to the first. It says:

"The Communist creed has the immense emotional appeal of a secular religion, whereas democracy, freedom of the individual, etc., have become stale *clichés*. If we want to counter the Communist threat, we must invent some revolutionary ideology or creed of a dynamic power equal to theirs."

Here we are again faced with the confusion between the desirable and the possible. Of course, if we had a flowing banner over us, like early Christianity or the Tricolore in 1789, all our troubles would be over. But a faith, whether religious or secular cannot be synthesised in a laboratory. Socialism, in one form or another, seemed the most promising secular religion until its atmosphere became corrupted, and its forces sapped, by Stalinism. In France and Italy, the worshippers of tyranny and terror usurp the rightful place of a truly progressive party and cunningly divert the energies of the progressive-minded into "anti-Fascist" crusades against coca-cola and General Franco—as if the threat to Europe came from Spain, not Russia, and the world had stood still since 1936.

As long as this encroachment lasts, there is no room on the French and Italian Left for the growth of a healthy progressive movement, and no chance for the development of a new, dynamic creed. The same is true, for different reasons, of British Labour's "Socialism in one country" policy. To set one's hopes on a European revival from these quarters means to indulge in wishful thinking of an entirely honourable, but unrealistic kind.

3

We conclude that the Communist expansion in Europe cannot be halted either by economic progress, however desirable in itself, nor by the invention of some miraculous patent ideology. Our time has no economic or spiritual panacea to offer the disheartened masses in Europe. How, then, can we expect them to recover faith in themselves?

There is only one way, the obvious way: to replace their shattered national consciousness and tottering loyalties to their rulers by a European consciousness and a European loyalty.

According to a recent poll conducted in twelve Western European countries, 54 per cent. of the people questioned were in favour of a Union of European nations, 38 per cent. were undecided, and only 8 per cent. against. In isolationist Britain, 51 per cent. were in favour of Union and only 9 per cent. against. Thus the answer to our question is given by the people of Europe themselves. They know by instinct that unification would mean infinitely more than a pooling of coal and steel, or the arithmetical addition of military forces. They know and feel that, almost regardless of immediate material benefits, the unification of Europe would provide precisely that emotional appeal and dynamic uplift, that return of self-confidence and resurrection of the European spirit, which is required to counter and defeat the Communist phantom creed.

In 1940, after the fall of Paris, Winston Churchill proposed the unification of the French and British Empires by a simple stroke of the pen. When the danger was past, the lesson was forgotten. In 1948, after Stalin's seizure of Czechoslovakia, Ernest Bevin declared that Europe must unite or perish. Since then, he and his colleagues have acted as if they had chosen the second alternative. Political federation, we have been told, is premature; it must be preceded by economic integration. But when the Schuman plan of economic integration was presented, it was declared inacceptable because it would entail a sacrifice in political sovereignty. And so it goes on.

Where can we break this vicious circle? The only political reality which has emerged after years of sterile haggling and prostration, is the Atlantic Pact. To the people of Europe this is still an abstract reality. A military alliance in itself is not a factor likely to ignite public imagination. But it could be made into such a factor.

A united European army could be the leaven which ultimately gives rise to a united Europe. It could be the means to by-pass the difficulties, real or imaginary, which at present block the road to political and economic integration. But on one condition only: that the problem of the European army should be approached not from a purely military, but from a psychological angle.

An army can reflect itself in the public mind as an abhorrent war-machine, or as a symbol which arouses the political libido and evokes fervent emotions. The armies of the French and American Revolutions, and the International Brigades in Spain, were such symbols. Is it very paradoxical to suggest that a European army of this type would be the most direct and logical means to restore Europe's faith in itself; to make it re-conquer its pride and dignity; and fill its people with a new, European consciousness?

4

In the first World War it took four years until the Western allies achieved unified command. In the second World War it again took more than four years. Last week, though the third World War has not yet started and may never start, the North Atlantic foreign ministers accepted Dean Acheson's proposal of a single military command, with authority to organise an "effective integrated force" of the twelve Western nations. This is an important step which seems to prove that, under the impact of the common danger, integration in the military field may be less difficult to achieve than in the economic and political field.

Naturally, there is still a very long way from a paper-resolution to practical reality. But here again a possible short-cut offers itself. It does not represent a solution to the problem of how to create an army out of units with different national allegiances, or to the problem of French anxieties regarding German rearmament—to mention only two of the obvious difficulties. The proposal I am going to make is merely an experiment; but an experiment relatively easy to carry out, which does not run counter to any vested national interests, and which, if successful, may produce far-reaching and unexpected results.

5

The proposal aims at the creation of an élite force, within the framework of the Atlantic Pact and under the direct authority of its supreme command, called the Legion of Liberty. The Legion of Liberty (abbrev. "LL"), is to consist of individual volunteers from the eleven West-European nations, and is to be so composed that the various nationalities are mixed together on the lowest level, i.e. that each platoon comprises soldiers from several, and if possible all, nationalities. In other words, instead of being "integrated from above" by the co-ordination of units from different national armies, the LL would be a force "integrated at the base". It would represent Pan Europa in a nutshell.

The value of such a force would be both practical and symbolic. Let us take the practical aspect first.

(a) The conventional units of the national armies which are to be "allocated" to the European command will have to be handled with due regard to the susceptibilities of the various powers concerned; friction, jealousies and resentment are un-avoidable in such cases. The LL units, on the other hand, would be at the immediate and direct disposal of the supreme command, and all diplomatic considerations, with their deleterious effects on strategy, would be short-circuited.

(b) The example of the French Foreign Legion, the Spanish Tertio, and the International Brigades tends to show that the fighting morale of such mixed units is excellent, and often superior to that of normal units. The reason for this may be that the heterogeneous nature of such forces leaves less scope than in homogeneous units for the development of collective grudges and adverse political currents.

(c) The language of command in the LL should be French. The language barrier presents no difficulties, as experience shows that the limited technical vocabulary of the army is picked up by the alien recruit almost as quickly as if he had to learn the terms in his own language. This the present writer can confirm from personal experiences as a soldier in the French Foreign Legion and the British Aliens' Pioneer Corps.

(d) Whereas the building up of the European army out of the "allocated" national contingents will require difficult negotiations and considerable time, the recruitment of one or several LL regiments could start immediately. The only condition required is that the various governments concerned should consider service in the Legion of Liberty as equivalent to military service at home. It is hard to see what valid objection could be raised to such an arrangement.

(e) The creation of the LL force does not interfere with existing official projects, such as the Acheson plan, or with un-official suggestions such as Churchill's Strasbourg proposal of a European Ministry of Defence, or the Culbertson proposal of a United Nations Police Force, or the proposal of Senator Lodge for a Brigade composed of refugees from Eastern Europe.

(f) The LL force should be modelled on the pattern of the U.S.A. "Regimental Combat Teams". That is to say, the LL regiment, or regiments (depending on the number of volunteers) should be to a large extent self-supporting, with their own infantry, tank and engineer battalions, field artillery, and a small tactical air arm.

The Legion should have American equipment and European manpower.

Its non-commissioned officers and subalterns should be selected according to ability; its officers from the rank of Captain upward should be citizens of small nations.

It should be stationed anywhere in Europe, e.g. in Western Germany or in the Franco-German border provinces.

6

The psychological aspect of the project, which is its very essence and *raison d'être*, need not be discussed at length. The very name of a "Legion of Liberty" expresses its symbolic value and emotional significance.

At worst, the LL would remain a small élite corps of a few thousand men—say 4000 to 5000, the strength of a single regiment. It is hard to imagine that this number of volunteers would not be forthcoming. Even on this limited scale its symbolic value would be considerable. The young men of various nationalities would, through mutual contact, gain an inestimable experience and enlarged horizon—much more effectively than through all sorts of summer schools, student exchange projects and holidays abroad. They would acquire a European consciousness, and spread it in their home countries after their return.

At best, the Legion of Liberty would become the catalytic agent for a truly integrated European Army, and thus the pioneer of a United Europe. Every squad, platoon and company would act as an incubator of the new European spirit. The condition of being a soldier would lose its odious associations with wars of national jealousy and imperialist conquest. The Legion of Liberty would discard the worn-out flags which have long ceased to represent the reality of our shrinking planet. The French *poilu* and the German *Soldat* would no longer regard themselves as the helpless victims of archaic chauvinism, or the sinister machinations of bankers and politicians. They would be soldiers of Europe, marching under the flag of Europe, to the sound of a European anthem.

"Why", wrote the President of the European Assembly, Henri Spaak, a few days ago, "why should the responsible statesmen who signed the Brussels Pact and the North Atlantic Treaty be incapable of drawing the logical conclusions from their texts? The defence of Europe means, to be sure, a good army; but it also means, and perhaps above all, the consciousness that Europe exists and that it deserves to exist."

POSTSCRIPT 1955

The plan proposed in this article was taken up by a group of American politicians, including some of General Eisenhower's close advisers. As the following excerpt (*New York Herald Tribune*, March 18, 1951) shows, it was for a while favourably discussed in Washington—and has apparently petered out since.

EISENHOWER'S MILITARY MELTING POT
3 Plans Studied for Integrating Nationalities in Army
By Vic Reinemer, Washington

. . . Military leaders, now that General Eisenhower has set up his cadre in Europe, will tackle in earnest the problem of finding the best way of

The European Legion

welding the soldiers from the North Atlantic pact countries into a cohesive and strong force.

Several types of military organisation may be considered. . . .

. . . A third proposal, favoured privately by some authorities but not widely publicised, is that the soldiers from all the Atlantic pact countries be mixed down through squad level, rather than separated in large national contingents. This may be more practicable and advantageous than it seems at first glance. Interviewed recently in Washington, officers from countries which have thus integrated soldiers from various language and cultural backgrounds, almost unanimously favoured such organisation over separation of the different groups.

Some advocates of this "tight" integration say a feasible way of initiating it would be to form an "Atlantic Legion" of volunteers from the Atlantic countries, responsible to SHAPE. . . . Such an Atlantic Legion, they say, would help unify the Atlantic community and serve as a pilot project for further, similar integration.

In some cases the language and cultural groups now united by this "man-to-man" method are more diverse than are those in the Atlantic area. For example, the Israeli Army includes immigrants from about fifty countries. Even now some of the recruits do not speak Hebrew, the official language. Yet they are mixed indiscriminately in the army. A ranking Israeli officer said that this "melting-pot" characteristic of the army has been the main unifier of the Israeli people.

In the South African Army Afrikaans (a Dutch idiom) is the mother tongue of slightly more than half the soldiers, English of the rest. Many recruits are not bilingual. Yet all are mixed, down through squad level, without regard for language. According to Brigadier J. B. Kriegler, the Union of South Africa's military attaché in Washington who served as director of military training in his country during World War II, this close association develops fast friendships and better relations between the two groups. . . .

A captain in the French Foreign Legion (in which many nationalities are mixed down through squad level) and an Israeli colonel both said that after about three months of combined military and language training their recruits without previous knowledge of the language of command know enough of it for ordinary military purposes. . . .

The Swiss Air Force uses a technical jargon which combines the country's three main languages, German, French and Italian. A Swiss air officer who used to command a squadron which included one

Italian, three French and six German speaking pilots said their diversity of ideas and temperaments made for a better staff organisation than did the relatively similar characteristics of one language and cultural group. . . .

Strained relations sometimes developed among the Allies during World War II when one national contingent suffered heavy casualties while others were comparatively unscathed. On the other hand, in a platoon or company which includes several nationalities, the common sacrifice tends to unite the troops, say men who have served in such units. . . .

The Atlantic peoples might well discover, as did the Israelis, that an army integrated on a man-to-man basis can infuse its *esprit de corps* into the entire life of the community. The creation of an Atlantic Legion could well be that big first step which would start the ball rolling.

A Guide to Political
Neuroses*

MOST CONTEMPORARY theories regarding political behaviour are based on a curious paradox. It is common knowledge (a) that crowds tend to behave in an irrational manner ("mass hysteria", "mass obsessions", etc.). It is equally common knowledge (b) that individuals often react in an irrational manner to the problems of sex and in their relations to family, superiors, and subordinates. Yet, while we admit that crowds behave like neurotics in public affairs, and that individuals display complexes in their private affairs, we still cling to the strange illusion that the average citizen, when not in a crowd, is a politically rational being. Our whole manner of running a democracy is based on this implicit assumption. This unwarranted, dogmatic belief in the political rationality of the individual is the ultimate reason why democracies are always on the defensive against totalitarian opponents, not only physically but also psychologically. For the evidence suggests that twentieth-century man is a political neutrotic.

The totalitarians have understood this from the beginning. They are the forces of death assailing our civilisation; and as death thrives on disease, he is a good diagnostician. If we want to survive, we must be equally good diagnosticians. But one cannot arrive at a correct diagnosis if one starts with the assumption

* First published in *Encounter*, November, 1953.

that the patient is sane. The belief in the basic political sanity and rationality of the individual has been implanted in us, during the Age of Enlightenment, by a long succession of French, German, and English philosophers—by Encyclopædists, Marxists, Benthamites, Owenites, and Progressives of all shades. Freud and his successors have demolished one corner of this optimistic belief in man as a rational being: we accept the fact that our sexual libido is thwarted. It is time for us to recognise that our political libido is just as complex-ridden, repressed and twisted, if not even more.

The Mental Curtain

At first sight it may seem that talk of a "political libido," a "political unconscious" and its "repressed memories," is merely a new intellectual pastime, a juggling with metaphors and analogies. But any detached study of the contemporary scene will show that the neurotic entanglements of the political instinct are as real, and no less profound, than those of the sexual instinct.

A neurotic may be described as a person who has faulty contact with reality, and whose judgments are based, not on hard facts, but on his wishes and fears. Facts which are likely to upset the patient's wish-and-fear universe are not admitted to consciousness; they are "censored" and become repressed complexes. If this simplified schema is applied to political behaviour, it will be seen to cover the whole range of political pathology, from the "controlled schizophrenia" of a Klaus Fuchs, through the wish-dream world of the Stockholm peace campaigner, to the flight from reality of the "neutralist". The political clichés which serve as rationalisations of his unconscious fears are as irrelevant as a neurotic's explanations of why he won't eat fish. When Harold Laski wrote to Mr. Justice Frankfurter in 1941 that "the U.S.S.R. has its roots in popular opinion more profound than any other system," argument had become pointless against such vagaries of the political libido, and the professor had become an obvious case for the psychotherapist.

Into the neurotic's distorted universe no facts are admitted which may upset its inner consistency. Arguments cannot penetrate the buffers of casuistry, the semantic shock-absorbers, the emotional defences. The inner censor—in the full psychiatric sense of the word—that protects the patient's illusions against the intrusion of reality, is incomparably more effective than any totalitarian state censorship. The political neurotic carries his private Iron Curtain inside his skull.

The unpalatable facts which have been rejected by the inner censor are subsequently repressed, and cluster into complexes. The political subconscious has its own logic, symptoms, and symbols. Alger Hiss and Whittaker Chambers have become such symbols in a Punch-and-Judy show or dream-fantasia, where guilt is attributed, not on the strength of evidence, but according to the dream-logic of the unconscious. If "censored" facts are mentioned in the presence of the political neurotic, he will react either with vehemence or a superior smile, either with straight abuse or with devious double-think, according to the nature of the defence-mechanism which protects him against his deep uncertainty and unconscious fear. Otherwise, the precarious balance of his dream-world would collapse and leave him defenceless against the stark world of reality—a reality so terrifying that even the sane can only face it with a shudder.

Repressed Guilt

In the gas chambers of Auschwitz, Belsen, and other extermination camps, around six million human beings were put to death during the closing phase of the Second World War. It was the greatest organised mass-killing in history. At the time it happened, the majority of the German people did not know what was going on. Since then, official documents, books and films have made the facts public to such an extent that it has become impossible for any educated person to ignore them. And yet the average German does manage to ignore them. The truth has not penetrated the nation's consciousness, and probably never will—because it is too terrifying to face. If admitted to consciousness, the load of guilt would be too heavy to carry, and would crush the nation's pride, frustrate its effort to rise again as a great European power. Many intelligent and well-meaning Germans react, when Auschwitz and Belsen are mentioned in their presence, with a stony silence and the pained expression of a Victorian lady confronted with a rude reminder of the Facts of Life: that they happen to be facts, never enters her head; they are just unmentionable, and that is all there is to them. Others will either deny the facts, or call them vastly exaggerated, or will, in the same breath, use several mutually contradictory arguments without being aware of the contradiction.

The remarkable thing about this reaction-pattern is that it betrays an unconscious guilt-complex even among those who had no share in the killings—and these are the vast majority of the Germans. Before the law, and as far as their conscious knowledge goes, they are innocent. To make a nation collectively responsible for the deeds of a criminal minority is both legally and morally unjust. But the "political subconscious" approaches the matter in a different way. It automatically assumes a shared collective responsibility in the nation's triumphs and defeats, in its honour and guilt. In fact, the most outstanding characteristic of the political libido is its tendency to identify the self with a nation, tribe, church, or party. The political libido can be defined as the individual's need to feel himself as part of a community, his urge to belong.

Now when this unconscious tendency towards identification produces pleasurable results, these are willingly admitted to the

conscious self: every German feels proud of "our Goethe" as if he
had a share in creating him, every American feels satisfaction
about the War of Independence as if he had fought in it. But the
less pleasurable products of the tendency towards identification
occupy no such place of honour in the conscious ego. And still
others may act as a traumatic shock, and therefore must be quickly
forgotten and repressed. *Our* Goethe, *our* Beethoven, *my* country
are part and parcel of the ego. But *our* Auschwitz, the children
whom *we* gassed, the war which *we* started, must be forced into
the mental underground.

Repressed political complexes have a thwarting effect, just
as repressed sexual complexes have. A lasting cure can only be
effected if the repressed experience is brought back to memory,
however painful the process may be. In the case under discussion,
this operation of mental hygiene could only be accomplished by
the leaders of the German people. Punishment and humiliation
inflicted from outside only make things worse. For the victors
it is right to forget; but the vanquished must learn to remember.

Collective Amnesia

The French suffer from a repressed complex of a different
kind, of which the manifestations are even more conspicuous.
When the legitimate government of France, after the collapse of
its armies, capitulated in June, 1940, the majority of Frenchmen
accepted the defeat and tried to reach some kind of *modus vivendi*
with the German victors. With Europe gone and England hopelessly isolated, this was for the average, non-political Frenchman
the only reasonable course to take. When General de Gaulle
proclaimed from London that "France had lost a battle but had
not lost the war," the people trapped in France understood that
this was a nice propaganda slogan, but had little relation to the
facts. For approximately two years they went about their business

as best they could, and enjoyed relative peace. Only a small number among them followed de Gaulle's call and escaped to England to enlist in his volunteer army, or joined the resistance movement. This again is only natural, for at the time resistance seemed sheer madness or quixotry, and at all times in all nations the heroic madmen have been a tiny minority.

The turning of the tide of war, the forced enlistment of Frenchmen for labour service in Germany, and a number of related factors gradually swelled the ranks of the resistance movement until, at the time of the Allied landing, some 20,000 to 40,000 Frenchmen were seriously engaged in sabotage, espionage, and armed resistance. Even at that time they were a small minority, and their bravery and self-sacrifice did not materially affect the course of the war. France was liberated not by the *maquis* but by the power of the Anglo-American war-machine, by British and American aircraft and tanks.

This hard fact was slurred over by the Anglo-American leaders who, for reasons of courtesy, vastly over-emphasised the French contribution to the war. It is only natural that French generals and politicians took the same line, in order to bolster up the nation's shaken self-respect and save it from the humiliating awareness of having been liberated by foreigners. Thus, within less than a year, the average Frenchman became honestly convinced that France had never been defeated, that she had been saved by her own effort, and moreover that he, Monsieur Dupont, had always been a valiant *résistant* and had only been lacking in opportunity to prove it. The memories of his own thoughts and acts during the dark interlude between 1940 and 1943 have been so successfully repressed that those years have become a kind of gap or hole in the texture of French history. This explains how it became possible for the French Communists, who from 1939 to 1941 had openly preached treason and surrender, and had called resistance to the German aggression an "imperialist adventure" and a "rich man's war," to emerge four years later as the strongest party in France. They benefited from the collective amnesia; their record was swallowed by the gap in the nation's memory.

Thus the mental structure of present-day France is built on delusion and self-delusion. The legend of the undefeated, victorious nation was first maintained by mutual tacit consent, then quickly grew into an act of faith. The former collaborator not only wears the ribbon of the *résistance* in his buttonhole; he also honestly believes that he is entitled to wear it. Because he admires the heroes of the resistance movement, and because he feels that they represent the true spirit of the nation, he is unconsciously led to believe that he belongs to them. It is *our* Goethe, *our* Jeanne d' Arc, *we* the nation of heroic *maquisards* all over again.

We see here a similar process at work as in the case of the Germans—the process of unconscious identification with a representative minority—but with opposite results. In the case of the Germans, identification resulted in shared guilt, which had to be repressed. In the case of the French, identification leads to shared glory, and allows the political libido to expand with a flourish. But the repressed memories exert their steady, poisonous influence on the nation's morale. The fiction of the past can only be maintained by evading the reality of the present. France, so the legend goes, owed nobody anything in the past, and will owe nobody anything in the future. If Marshall Aid is sent to her, this is done to serve some obscure scheme of Wall Street. If arms and troops are sent, it is to further the interests of American imperialism. The only war-time memories connected with Americans which have remained vivid and undistorted are that the bombers often missed their targets, destroying French cities and lives; and that G.I.s often got drunk and traded cigarettes for the passing favours of women. Hence: no more liberation *à l'Américaine*. We want to be left alone. We want none of your alms, and none of your coca-cola, and none of your atom-bombs. If you leave us alone, the Russians will leave us alone too.

Elaborate variations of this theme can be read every day in French newspapers of all shades. The one subject never mentioned is the tragic but crucial fact that the physical survival of France depends on the American atomic potential. If it were admitted, the whole fictitious structure would collapse. And if one were to take away the wishful element from the patient's wish-and-fear world, only fear would remain—the unbearable, repressed terror of a Europe still virtually defenceless against the Russian threat.

So the fiction has to be maintained, and reality evaded at all cost. This is not conscious hypocrisy, nor ingratitude, and it implies no slight on the French character. Any nation which has suffered three invasions within one century and lost at least one male member per family, would develop the same neurotic pattern.

Escape from Reality

Escape from reality is a basic feature of contemporary Europe, but has for a long time been a specific British vice. It almost seems as if the British had paid for their remarkable immunity from hysteria by imperviousness to reality; a short-coming craftily hidden by the art of making their follies appear as sweet reasonableness.

In the days of the London blitz, the P.E.N. Club had asked Louis Golding to give a talk comparing the American to the British novel. Golding had just finished when the air-raid warning went, but the discussion was continued, business as usual. The second or third speaker was a crumpled, tweedy, lovable little man who, I believe, had written a biography of an obscure Wiltshire naturalist of the 17th century. He was attacking Hemingway, Dos Passos, Faulkner, and others.

A Guide to Political Neuroses

"It seems to me," he gently explained, "that these modern American novelists suffer from a morbid preoccupation with violence. When you read their books you would think that the ordinary man spends his life punching people's noses or being hit on the head. Now, as a matter of fact, ordinary people rarely meet with violence in their lives. They get up in the morning, potter in their gardens. . . . "

A bomb whistled and crashed some blocks away, and the anti-aircraft batteries started their infernal hollering. The little man waited patiently for the next lull, then calmly continued:

"What I mean to say is, violence rarely plays a part in ordinary people's lives, and it is positively indecent for an artist to devote so much time and space to that kind of thing. . . . "

One of the outstanding features of neurotic behaviour is the patient's inability to learn from his past experiences. As if acting under a spell, he gets himself again and again into the same type of entanglement and repeats the same errors. British foreign policy towards European union, and French internal politics during the last thirty years, seem to be dictated by this kind of repetition-compulsion.

The trigger which set off the Second World War was Germany's claim to a town that formed an enclave in Polish territory and could only be reached through a corridor. That war was not yet over when Allied statesmen agreed to create a new enclave of exactly the same type, only accessible through a corridor across foreign territory. The name of the first enclave was Danzig; the name of the second is Berlin. Behind the shallow truism that "History repeats itself" hide the unexplored forces which lure men into repeating their own tragic errors.

The obvious and outstanding example of such a compulsion is the so-called policy of appeasement. The lesson of the '30s: that an aggressive, expansive power with a messianic belief in its

223

mission will expand as long as a power-vacuum exists; that improvement of social conditions, however desirable in itself, is no deterrent and no protection against attack; that the price of survival is the sacrifice of a distressing part of the national income for defence over a distressingly long period; and that appeasement, however seductive and plausible its arguments sound, is not a substitute for military strength but a direct invitation to war— all this should be still only too fresh in our memories; yet an astonishing number of politicians, not to mention the millions of common men, seem determined to commit the same errors, and re-live the same tragedy again.

"From the danger of war one cannot protect oneself by weapons, one can achieve this only by moving forward into a new world of law. . . . Armaments cannot be fought by piling up armaments; that would be like getting Beelzebub to drive out the Devil."

This sounds like a speech by Mr. Aneurin Bevan in 1953. In fact it is a speech by Mr. Clement Attlee, delivered on 11th March, 1935 in the House of Commons in protest against the Government's proposal of a modest increase in rearmament.* When he suggested "disbanding the national armies" as a brilliant idea to save peace, he was interrupted by shouts "Tell that to Hitler". He brushed the interruption aside, as Mr. Bevan brushes similar irrelevancies aside eighteen years later. In the same year, 1935, a "Peace Ballot" obtained eleven million signatures in England —more than half the English electorate. All this is forgotten today, repressed and relegated to the political subconscious.

Even the slogans by which the aggressor hypnotised the victim were the same. Hitler sponsored Peace Congresses of German and French war veterans who protested against the conspiracy of the

* Obviously, one could find similar statements by Conservative spokesmen of other periods.

"cannon merchants" and the pluto-democractic warmongers of Wall Street. Anti-Nazi refugees who talked about Hitler's concentration camps and aggressive intentions were regarded as atrocity-mongers, persecution maniacs, and fomenters of hatred between nations, as their successors, Russian refugees and ex-Communists, are regarded to-day. If only the Cassandras and Jeremiahs would shut up, all would be well! After each act of aggression, Hitler made a gesture of peace which was as eagerly taken at face value as are similar gestures by Stalin and Malenkov; men who warned against such gullibility were accused of deliberately sabotaging the chances of peaceful settlement. The scapegoat, the "real warmonger," was at that time not the U.S.A. but— France. When Duff Cooper, then Minister for War, made a speech strongly emphasising Franco-British friendship, he was attacked by Labour in both Houses, and Mr. Attlee pointed out that "such strong emphasis on friendship with one country induces other countries (i.e. Germany) to wonder why they are not addressed with similar friendship". When Hitler marched into the Rhineland (and immediately afterwards offered a twenty-five years' peace pact), the French Prime Minister came to London, and had the same type of welcome that American generals have nowadays in France. Detached political experts who did not like the Nazi régime warned against exaggerating its dangers by pointing out that the Germans only wanted to annex German territories such as the Rhineland and the Saar, but were "far too intelligent" to swallow a foreign body like Czechoslovakia, which they could never digest. Since 1945, we hear precisely the same argument regarding Russia's intentions in Central and Western Europe.

The result of all this was that by 1936 the Belgians, Rumanians, Yugoslavs, etc., had become "neutralists" and the system of collective security disintegrated as N.A.T.O. is disintegrating to-day.

The Failure of Response

The neurotic who each time commits the same type of error and each time hopes to get away with it is not stupid; he is just ill.

Some Minor Aberrations

For nearly every aberration of the sexual drive we can find a corresponding type of disturbance of the political libido. I shall mention only a few of the most prevalent patterns of political neurosis.

A person may both love and hate another person, and experience these emotions either simultaneously or in alternation—as in the case of temperamental couples, or of difficult child-parent relations. A typically ambivalent relationship of this kind exists between Britain and the U.S.A. Americans both love and deride English aristocrats, fashions, accents, and the stuffiness of British traditions in general. The British, for different reasons, view America with equally mixed feelings of admiration and mockery, envy and contempt. About once in every six months Anglo-American relations get poisoned and there is a minor crisis—mostly caused, not by any real conflict of interests, but by the mutual exasperation typical in an ambivalent partnership.

It also happens in neurotic case-histories that an emotion is succeeded in a lasting fashion by its opposite: blind infatuation by blind hatred, fervent admiration by shuddering revulsion. Many ex-Communists, ex-Catholics, and ex-patriates fall into this attitude of the disappointed lover towards the party, church, or country which once meant everything to them.

Fetishism

In psychiatric parlance, this means an aberration whereby the sexual instinct becomes attached to a symbol, or accessory, or part, of its natural object. Women's locks, or corsets, or

226

riding-boots, may become the object of fetishist worship. Exactly the same fate may befall the political libido.

The fetish-character of such symbols as flags, uniforms, emblems, songs, and anthems is too obvious to need emphasis. In an equally obvious way, propaganda exploits such characteristic features as Hitler's forelock, Churchill's cigar, Stalin's high-necked tunic. Though the existence of such mass-infatuations is known, they are rarely recognised as the pathological symptoms they are. They not only mean a regression to primitive idolatry and totem-worship, but also that the symbol or part which has become the object of the fetishist cult replaces the thing which it stands for, and thus deflects the social energy from its original aim. The political drive of millions of idealists who started on the quest for a better world has thus been perverted, the striving for progress turned into the worship of "the Party," which is no longer regarded as an accessory to the original purpose, but as an object of worship in its own right.

Eternal Adolescents

The young radical intellectual of Bloomsbury, St. Germain des Près, or Greenwich Village is a relatively harmless type. Often his radicalism is derived from adolescent revolt against the parents, or some other stereotyped conflict which makes him temporarily despair of the world. But some of the young radicals never grow up; they remain the eternal adolescents of the Left.

One variety of this type is frequently found both in the United States and in France, though rarely in England. Young X. starts as an enthusiastic Communist, is soon disillusioned, founds a Trotskyite opposition group of ten people, discovers that six out of the ten form a secret "opposition *bloc*" within the group, is disillusioned, founds a little "mag" with a hundred per cent. anti-capitalist, anti-Stalinist, anti-pacifist programme, goes bankrupt, starts a new little mag, and so on. All his struggles, polemics, victories, and defeats are storms in a teacup, confined to the same small circle of radical intellectuals—a kind of family which thrives on quarrels and mutual denunciations, and yet coheres by virtue of some unique dialectical glue. A classic example is the group of Marxist-Existentialists around Sartre's *Les Temps Modernes*, with their perennial quarrels and schisms. The sectarian may be said to suffer from the *incestuous* type of political libido.

A different type is Y., the busybody, whose name is on every "progressive" committee, whose voice is raised in protest against every injustice, who has embraced every good cause under the sun, and has never achieved anything on earth. Y. is the political equivalent of a *nymphomaniac*; he suffers from an excess of political libido. This kind of neurosis, too, flourishes chiefly in the climate of the Left—for, generally speaking, the Left is politically over-sexed.

Finally there is Z., the political *masochist*. With him, the parable of the mote and the beam has been reversed. The slightest injustice in his own country wrings from him cries of anguish and despair, but he finds excuses for the most heinous crimes committed in the opposite camp. When a coloured tennis-player is refused a room in a London luxury hotel, Z. quivers with spontaneous indignation; when millions spit out their lungs in Soviet Arctic mines and lumber-camps, Z.'s sensitive conscience is silent. Z. is an inverted patriot, whose self-hatred and craving for self-punishment has turned into hatred for his country or social class, and a yearning for the whip that will scourge it.

The Desire to Belong

It is a truism of psychiatry that nobody is perfectly sane. The difference between a normal person and a neurotic is a difference in degree, not in kind. But in specific periods of history, the social and cultural climatic favours specific trends towards neurosis and aberration. In golden-age Greece, male homosexuality was an almost general phenomenon. In the 1920s, promiscuity reached unprecedented proportions. The political libido has similar ups and downs, ranging from relative normality to near-insanity. For a considerable time now we have been witnessing a steady deterioration towards the latter.

The possible causes of this process can only be briefly alluded to. While the sexual drive serves to perpetuate the race, the political libido represents the individual's urge to identify himself with an idea, or a set of values embodied in a community—in other words, his need "to belong". Both are basic human instincts, though during the last few decades the importance of the second has been somewhat obscured by the Freudians' exclusive emphasis on the first.

In medieval days, despite wars, famines, and epidemics, man lived in a relatively stable universe. The formidable authority of the church, the fixed hierarchy of the medieval state, the belief in providence and divine justice, gave people a feeling of security and belonging. Then came a series of earthquakes, starting with the Renaissance, continued during the Reformation, and culminating in the French and Russian Revolutions, which gradually but completely shattered man's outlook on society and the universe. Medieval life had been regulated by unchallengeable commands, each ending with an exclamation mark; now all these were turned into question marks. The whole earth, formerly the stable centre of the universe, was transformed into a swirling experimental laboratory; values crumbled, ties snapped, the political libido of man was turned loose like an adolescent's erotic cravings. But up to this day the quest for a new, comprehensive order and creed which would embrace man's relation *both* to the universe and to society, has remained without result. Twentieth-century man is a political neurotic because he has no answer to the question of the meaning of life, because socially and metaphysically he does not know where he "belongs".

According to circumstances, a frustrated instinct may manifest itself in a great variety of forms, and contradictory symptoms are often found in the same person. Prolonged frustration and defeat may lead to an atrophy of the instinct—the patient becomes socially apathetic, his disappointments turn into political cynicism and anti-social behaviour. Symptoms of this process, of the political libido turning sour, can be most strikingly observed in contemporary France.

Even more dangerous is the opposite process. The unfulfilled urge "to belong" may lead to "political oversexedness," expressing itself in blind, self-sacrificing devotion to some unholy cause. In our age those who felt most deeply that paradise was lost, were the first to be attracted by the *ersatz*-kingdoms of heaven: the World Revolution, Soviet Russia, or the Thousand-Year-Reich. In psychiatric language, they developed "fixations" of their political libido towards these gory substitutes for Utopia.

All this does not mean that one should underestimate the importance of economic factors and social pressures. No psychiatrist can cure poverty and disease among the vast populations of Asia. But the crucial point is that before the economic needs of people express themselves in political action, a mental process intervenes; and this mental process, as often as not, initiates action directly *opposed* to the original need. The optimistic thinkers of the 19th century thought that, by and large, the actions of the masses coincided with their interests; the 20th century reminded us that even highly civilised people like the Germans are capable of committing collective suicide, driven by some neurotic obsession, and regardless of economic reality.

Reasoning alone does not help against such obsessions. It is in the nature of totalitarian creeds that they provide the believer with emotional saturation, a complete experience of belonging. Politicians are supposed to have a smattering of history and economics; it is time they were obliged to learn the elements of psychology, and to study the strange mental forces which compel people to act with such stubborn determination against their proper interests.

The Trail of the Dinosaur

1

LET US imagine a kind of temperature-chart on which the growing power of *homo sapiens* over his environment is represented by a curve. For something of the order of half a million years, from Java Man to about 5000 B.C., the curve would remain nearly static, represented by a roughly horizontal line. With the invention of the pulley, the lever, and a few simple mechanical devices, the muscular strength of man would appear amplified, say, five-fold; and after that, the curve would again remain nearly horizontal for the next five or six thousand years. But in the course of the last three hundred years, the curve would, for the first time in the history of the species, rise steeply in leaps and bounds, until it pointed almost vertically upward. To draw this chart true to scale, we would have to use graph paper several miles long; even so we would have only an inch or less of the paper left to plot the sudden, dramatic lifting of the curve's head—like a cobra stabbing upward.

Another, more specific chart, representing the destructive potentialities of the growth of power, would look even more dramatic—one merely has to remember that after the first World War, only forty years ago, statisticians reckoned that on the average ten thousand rifle bullets or ten artillery shells were needed to kill one enemy soldier.

Now let us contrast these two charts with a third one, on which we plot the progress of the species Man in moral philosophy, in cosmic awareness and spiritual clarity. This curve will show a slow rise during the prehistoric miles of nearly-flat stretch; then, when the Power-curve (P) starts rising, the Spiritual curve (S) will begin to undulate with indecisive ups and downs; finally, on the last, dramatic one-millionth part of the chart, where the P-curve shoots skyward with insane acceleration, the S-curve goes into a steep decline. The spiritual void at the end of the chart is less obvious than the accumulation of power: I shall come back to the "S-curve" later on.

The point of these imaginary charts is that they show a very unusual type of curve, a geometrical freak which forces us to measure time at first in units of hundred thousands, then of thousands of years, then in centuries and decades until, towards the end, a single year weighs more than ten thousand years did before. A process which, once past a critical limit, shows this type of catastrophic acceleration, is called, in Physics, an explosion. A dispassionate observer from another world, to whom centuries are as seconds, able to survey the whole curve in one sweep, would have to come to the conclusion that our civilisation is either on the verge of, or in the process of, exploding.

I would like to labour the geometrical aspect of human evolution a little further by suggesting two more curves, the first representing progress in communication (C), the second, progress in understanding (U). The C-curve, which would comprise travel, and communication by visual and acoustic means, would again remain nearly flat for aeons; then, with the invention of the printing press, the steamship, railway, motor car, gramophone, telephone, cinema, aeroplane, radio, video, radar and jukebox (all, except for the printing press, crowded into a single century) the curve would rise steeply to near-saturation—the point where the whole surface of the planet is visually and acoustically interconnected. One should have expected that this shrinking of the terrestrial surface in terms of communication would lead to a proportionate increase in its intellectual cohesion; but this did not happen. The shrinking of the distance between nations did not bring them "nearer" to each other; three-dimensional travel did not abolish Chinese Walls and Iron Curtains, but merely extended them into atmospheric space; the unifying medium of the aether was split up by censorship and jamming. Even between such close neighbours and allies as the people of England and France, mutual comprehension and human sympathy is not markedly greater now than at a time when they were days, instead of hours, apart.

Nor did the extension of the range of the sense-organs through radio and television increase the intellectual range of the human mind, its powers of abstraction and synthesis. It seems rather that the reverse is true: that the stupendous amplification of vision and hearing caused a rapid deterioration of the intellectual and moral content of communication. In the new generation born into the age of television, not only the habit of reading, but the faculty of thinking in abstract, conceptual terms seems to be weakened by the child's conditioning to easier and more primitive forms of visual perception. The dangers of this regression from the conceptual to the perceptual, from abstract language to picture-strip language, are less obvious and immediate, but in the long run no less grave, than the spectacular increase in destructive power.

To sum up, our diagrams show an unprecedented increase in the range and power of the species' sensory and motor organs, coincident with a marked deterioration of the integrative functions which determine spiritual maturity and social ethics. There are frequent instances in history of moral slumps followed by a new upward trend; the alarming thing is the coincidence of a period of unprecedented spiritual decline with an equally unprecedented increase of power. The Promethean myth seems to be coming true with a horrible twist: the giant reaching out to steal the lightning from the gods is morally insane. Hence the difficulty as Bertrand Russell wrote a few years ago, "to persuade mankind to acquiesce in its own survival".

2

Any attempt at such persuasion must take both the short-term and the long-term aspects of the situation into account. The first is political, the second transcendental in nature; and the two interact more directly than we realise. The politician unaware of the transcendental background of the crisis can offer only makeshift measures; and the saint who remains aloof in an emergency sins by omission.

On the level of practical policy, it is essential to distinguish between the desirable and the possible. We know by now that atomic war would be tantamount to a collective suicide of the species. To abolish the threat of atomic war is certainly desirable, but not in the realm of the possible. The banning of atomic weapons can only be effective if both parties agree to international supervision under conditions which include permanent inspection—the throwing open of the locked doors of secret laboratories, factories, plants, mines and military installations. But such a policy runs counter to the tradition of secrecy and distrust which Russia and the Asiatic nations have practised for centuries past; and it also runs counter to the basic principles and political structure of all dictatorial régimes, Communist or other. A dictatorship that accepted democratic controls, internally or internationally, would cease to be a dictatorship. The Chinese Wall and the Iron Curtain are not accidents of history, but massive symbols of national traditions and social régimes whose existence depends on their ability to block the movement of people and ideas.

Even if the present rulers of Russia desired to submit to genuine international control and inspection, they could not afford to do so any more than they could afford to abolish censorship, the one-party system, the political police and other essential requisites of dictatorship. Whether the dictatorship is good or bad, whether it is a dictatorship of the workers, peasants or dentists, of a bureaucracy or a theocracy, is irrelevant in this context.

It is equally irrelevant under what pretexts the Soviet Government evades the issue of genuine inspection and control—whether by procedural subterfuges, or by rejecting "infringements of national sovereignty", or by spurious peace campaigns and the demand for a platonic ban on atomic weapons which would work against the side that manufactures and tests its bombs openly, and which would set a premium on secrecy. Oak Ridge, Harwell, Bikini, are widely discussed subjects in the West, while the corresponding places and events in the East are shrouded in complete secrecy.

I repeat: the abolition of atomic weapons under effective international control is entirely desirable, and by the nature of things just as impossible as it proved impossible to enforce disarmament in the defunct League of Nations' days. From this realistic starting point, three courses are open to the West. To continue developing nuclear weapons in full awareness of the danger to the human species; to renounce nuclear weapons one-sidedly, in full awareness of the decisive advantage thereby accorded to the opponent; or, finally, to start a "preventive" war (which is of course a contradiction in terms), based on the assumption that the West still possesses a decisive superiority in atomic weapons, that this advantage is being lost, and that war at the present level of atomic developments would be less devastating than war in five or ten years' time and would impose a lasting peace on a unified world.

The third possibility we must reject out of hand, on the grounds that it is based on the old Ends and Means fallacy (cf. "The Challenge of our Time"). All social progress, all human justice, requires a certain amount of ruthlessness; all surgical cures, the infliction of a certain amount of pain. But this justification of the means by the end is confined to very narrow limits, to situations where all the factors are of a manageable order and the results predictable with reasonable certainty—otherwise "the surgeon's lancet turns into the butcher's hatchet". With regard to preventive war, none of the above conditions is present. The amount of damage that would be inflicted on humanity is incalculable, the factors in the equation are unmanageable, and the results unpredictable. Even on the inadmissible premise that morality should be sacrificed to expediency, and the present generation sacrificed in the interest of future ones—even on these premises preventive war must be ruled out on the grounds that the magnitude and complexity of factors are beyond the computing capacity of the human brain.

Unfortunately, the premises that we reject are not rejected by the philosophy of dialectical materialism which is the *credo* of our opponents; and our scepticism regarding the limits of man's ability as a computing machine, is not shared by them. Thus the possibility that our opponents may start "preventive" war at a moment which they judge "historically favourable" and under any convenient pretext, cannot be ruled out.

I would like to make this point clearer. In the previous paragraph I was not concerned with the question whether certain members of the Politbureau think it practicable to start a war in six months or six years, or whether they think that the inevitable Communist World-State can be realised without war. My point is that their philosophical approach to, and their terms of reference regarding, the problem of war are different from ours. The West has no unified philosophy, but it has a long and continuous ethical tradition which more or less articulately, more or less consciously, permeates the thinking of both leaders and people and limits the formers' freedom of action. The leaders of the other side are not subject to such limitations either by the philosophy to which they adhere, or by the machinery of democratic control. It is an unequal contest where one side believes in its historic mission which justifies all means including war, whereas the other does not; where one party is bound by certain rules of the game, the other party is not.

This difference ought to be constantly present to the mind of all responsible politicians, Left or Right, and guide their decisions, large and small. But psychologically, this is a rather difficult thing to ask for, because the tactical oscillations of Soviet policy, the occasional easing of surface tensions, and the frequent unmannerliness of American politicians, tend to obscure and blur the basic difference in philosophy. Wishful thinking, infatuation with pious platitudes, and the tempting road of least resistance are constantly lessening the West's chances of survival.

3

Marxist theory teaches that the proletariat must exploit to the full the constitutional freedoms which bourgeois democracy is obliged to grant (for the bourgeoisie is bound to be "its own gravedigger") until an "objectively revolutionary situation" occurs. At that moment the proletariat will rise and inter its opponents in their self-prepared grave. *Mutatis mutandis* the same theory applies to the international scene, where the notion of the "objectively revolutionary situation" is replaced by the "historically favourable situation" for adding another vassal nation to the existing ones. One-sided atomic disarmament would automatically create a "historically favourable situation" for Russia's bid to unify the world after its own fashion in the interest of mankind.

There is nothing new about the argument that the only deterrent against atomic aggression is an atomic stockpile. But there is a new development regarding the value of an atomic stockpile against non-atomic, local aggression. The theory that the atomic superiority of the West could prevent local aggression by the threat of massive retaliation has become obsolete for two reasons: firstly, Western atomic superiority is on the wane; secondly, the destructive power of the new weapons is now so monstrous that the punishment of limited and camouflaged aggression by the unleashing of open atomic war has become politically and morally impossible. A policeman, armed with an atom bomb and nothing else, could not prevent the escape of a couple of housebreakers without blowing the whole town to glory, himself included. We are faced with a new paradox: the superior power of a weapon may reduce its bearer to helplessness.

The policeman's part is made even more difficult by the fact that political crimes are easier to camouflage than common burglaries. Russia has conquered one half of Europe and a large portion of Asia through acts of aggression in varying disguises of varying plausibility, none of which presented a clear-cut *casus belli*. The possibilities of veiled aggression are inexhaustible; and it is unrealistic to believe that we can stop it by the threat of "massive retaliation"—which, if taken seriously, would mean that we ought to have reacted to the defenestration of Masaryk, or ought to react to the next People's Rising in Afghanistan, by unleashing the nuclear nightmare.

The upshot of this argument is that policing the world and guaranteeing collective security never was, and never will be, possible through reliance on the West's industrial superiority and dreams of push-button retaliation. To put it in a nutshell: *atomic weapons are necessary as a deterrent against atomic aggression, but ineffective as a deterrent against local and camouflaged aggression.* The security of our streets cannot be guaranteed by tanks, only by police constables in sufficient numbers, armed with conventional weapons to cope with conventional crimes. The practical conclusions are distressingly simple. The most conventional of all weapons, and the one which no nation can dispense with, is a people determined to fight on the beaches and to fight in the streets in defence of their freedom. However brave they are, they will never be able to stand up against an aggressor using the methods of total war. But if they are strong enough, and brave enough, they will survive because of the aggressor's reluctance to engage in open, total war. The oft-heard argument: "What is the good of arming a few more divisions when we know that in the case of a showdown Europe cannot be defended anyway?" is both cowardly and false. Any European Defence Community can never aim at more than to make Europe unconquerable *short of total war*. But it can never aim at less than this. If, in the early post-war period, Czechoslovakia and Poland had been equipped with the number of divisions and the unbroken spirit of Finland in 1939, the Russians could not have deposed the Polish Government, nor pulled their Prague *coup*. They would have been forced to show their hand and engage in open warfare —and the odds are that they would not have dared to take the risk. It is indeed distressingly simple: free men must be prepared to defend their freedom or lose it.

4

The rearming of Western Germany is a side-issue which will probably be settled by the time this appears in print; but the passions raised by it will persist for some time and be exploited by the conscious and unconscious enemies of Western survival. The emotional resistance of the former victims of German militarism is understandable, but unfortunately beside the point; without German divisions Europe cannot be defended. The fear that the rearming of Western Germany may lead to a repetition of 1914 and 1939, reflects a humiliating inferiority complex and implies that Europe and the United States will repeat the mistakes which made German aggression possible. If the Atlantic Community cannot trust itself to keep under control a limited number of German divisions under unified command, then it has no chance to survive. It would of course be much preferable to have a European Army united "at the base", not "at the top" (cf. "The European Legion.") A quasi pan-European army with a pan-European spirit and flag is, I believe, not only desirable, but still in the realm of the possible.

5

At the beginning of this essay, I made a distinction between the short-term and long-term aspects of the present crisis. All that I have said so far, refers to the short-term aspect and to short-term measures. The best we can hope to achieve by these measures is to gain time. Even if courage and reason prevail to a much greater extent than in recent years, the result cannot be more than a strategic and economic patchwork on a divided planet.

And yet by gaining time, by prolonging this misery of co-existence, mankind may hope for a reprieve. The nature of this tenuous hope I have tried to explain in "An Outgrown Dilemma". It is based on the possibility of some unexpected mutation in man's dominating passions and interests. Whenever history became polarised between two competing power-centres, roughly one of two things happened. Either one of the contestants was subjugated (the Rome-versus-Carthage pattern); or a stalemate was reached (the Christianity-versus-Islam pattern). Such stalemates have always started as unstable and precarious forms of "co-existence", spotted with local outbreaks which threatened to grow into a total conflict. But under certain favourable conditions the stalemate became a permanent one, co-existence gradually changed into collaboration, and the crisis was over.

The conditions for this to happen are partly of a physical, partly of a psychological nature. The physical basis of the stalemate is balance of power, both "central" and "peripheral". By "central" power I mean the total strength which each side would be capable of throwing into a total showdown, and which acts as a mutual deterrent from risking such a showdown. By "peripheral" strength I mean the physical and moral capacity of exposed outposts and enclaves to defend themselves and hold out, if only for a limited time. This "peripheral" strength is essential to the balance, because it makes the potential aggressor realise that he cannot have his way *in a swift and discrete manner*, and thus multiplies the risks attached to aggression. The Christian enclaves in Jaffa and Acre during the Crusades, the Protestant enclaves in Catholic countries and *vice versa* after the Thirty Years War, seem to prove that a stalemate may extend to the oddest geographical patchwork if the above-mentioned conditions are fulfilled. The Night of St. Bartholomew carries such vivid memories because it was an exception, and not the rule. On the other hand, the fate of the Jewish minorities in Europe, and of the Armenian enclaves in Turkey, was a kind of St. Bartholomew in permanence, because there was neither a "central" power nor any peripheral strength to defend them.

However, a stalemate based on the balance of physical power is in itself not enough to prevent an ultimate showdown. The second condition is a change of the spiritual climate, a spontaneous mutation of interest, which blunts the horns of the dilemma. While the process of polarisation is at its height, it looks as if the whole world must either go Moslem or Christian, either Catholic or Protestant, either Monarchist or Republican, either Socialist or Capitalist. But if the deadlock lasts long enough, an unexpected mutation of the mass-mind may occur, the inevitable choice no longer appears inevitable, passion drains away and people simply become interested in something else. Religious consciousness yields to national consciousness, the fight for space to the fight for markets, the struggle between "Left" and "Right" to the struggle between East and West. The word "heretic" has now gone into metaphorical use, though once it meant torture and the stake; and whether we live under a King or a President, is the least of our worries. Over and again it happened in history that the dynamo which generates the light and the sparks was switched off just before the fuses blew. But in order that this may happen, some new dynamo must enter into action producing a different type of current, a shift of interest to a different set of values, conflicts and predicaments.

Every branch of human activity—literature, the arts, philosophy even medicine—seems to be subject to these unpredictable periodic mutations; see the sudden shifts of emphasis in painting from narrative to composition, from contour to surface, from the sculptural to the dynamic, from representational to geometrical. It is not fashion that changes but the focus of the eye and the mind, concentrating its attention on different aspects, in due turn, of the complex entity, man—religious man, economic man, *homo politicus, homo faber, homo liber.*

One of these changes of spiritual climate, which is of particular relevance to us, seems to have occurred somewhere half-way through the Thirty Years War. I am quoting from Miss Wedgwood's classic work on the subject★:

"Never had the Churches seemed stronger than in the opening decades of the seventeenth century. Yet a single generation was to witness their deposition from political dominance. The tragic results of applied religion had discredited the Churches as the directors of the State. A new

★ C. V. Wedgwood: *The Thirty Years War,* London, 1938.

emotional urge had to be found to fill the place of spiritual conviction; national feeling welled up to fill the gap. The terms Protestant and Catholic gradually lose their vigour, the terms German, Frenchman, Swede, assume a gathering menace. A new standard of right and wrong came into the political world. Insensibly and rapidly after that, the Cross gave place to the flag, and the 'Sancta Maria' cry of the White Hill to the 'Viva España' of Nördlingen."

Admittedly, by the time this great change came into the world, the war had run half its course and taken its toll of death and devastation; and it took another thirteen years to end. But perhaps the Russian conquest of Eastern Europe and the wars in Greece, China, Korea and Indo-China constitute the first half of our thirty years' war; and perhaps the second half need not be repeated—at least it may be argued, that the conflict between Bourbon and Hapsburg had little relation to the original religious issue.

6

The age of religious conflict was superseded in the course of the 17th century by the emergence of two apparently unrelated factors: the rise of national consciousness, and the rise of a new philosophy. The latter, based on the discoveries of Copernicus, Galileo and Kepler, was gradually penetrating wider and wider strata of the public mind. If the earth no longer stood firmly planted by God in the centre of His universe, and was merely a small planet hurtling through space, then, though religious belief did survive, it could no longer command the exclusive interest of man. The sky around him had remained the same, but the focus of his eyes had radically changed since he had learnt that the fixed stars of the firmament did not dance attendance to him, and were blinking down with detached irony at the tiny creature on his spinning cannon ball. Within a century, more or less, the mind of European man had undergone a mutation more radical and fraught with consequences than if he had acquired a third eye or an additional limb.

It was a historic turning-point—the point where religion and science, religion and art, logics and ethics, began to part company and go their own separate ways. From the beginnings of civilised life, man's fate had been determined, and his conscience guided, by some super-human agency; from now on this function was taken over by sub-human agencies. The deities of the past may have been coarse or sublime, scandalous Olympians or a pure God of love; yet they were wiser, more powerful and on a higher plane of existence than man himself. The new determinants of man's fate—mechanical laws, atoms, glands, genes—which gradually took over, were of a lower order than man himself; they defined his condition but could provide no guidance whatsoever for his conscience.

The consequences of this shift of "destiny from above" to "destiny from below"* became only gradually apparent. Before the shift, the various religions had provided man with explanations of a kind which gave to everything that happened to him meaning in the wider sense of a transcendental causality and a transcendental justice. But the explanations of the new philosophy were devoid of meaning in this wider sense. The answers of the past had been varied, contradictory, primitive, superstitious or whatever one likes to call them, but they had been firm, definite, imperative. They satisfied, at least for a given time and culture, man's need for reassurance and protection in an unfathomably cruel world, for some guidance in his perplexities. The new answers, to quote William James, "made it impossible to find in the driftings of the cosmic atoms, whether they work on the

* Cf. *The Yogi and the Commissar.* London, 1945.

universal or on the particular scale, anything but a kind of aimless weather, doing and undoing, achieving no proper history, and leaving no result".* In a word, the old explanations, with all their arbitrariness and patchiness, answered the question after "the meaning of life" whereas the new explanations, with all their precision, made the question of meaning itself meaningless.

Our thinking habits are so entirely conditioned by post-Copernican developments that we automatically assume thinking always to have followed the same method. We take the ethical neutrality of our "natural laws", the split between "religious" and "scientific" truth so much for granted that we assume they must have always existed. It requires a great imaginative effort to realise the full significance of the "shift of destiny" of three hundred years ago; and that it constitutes a new departure, a break in the curve of man's spiritual evolution as unprecedented and unique as the sudden vertiginous rise of his physical power. We don't know how many tens of thousand years ago man for the first time asked the question about the meaning of life; but we do know at what point, so close to us in time, he lost the answer to it.

7

For a long time the majority of mankind remained unaware of the implications of the new philosophy. Its pioneers talked in a timid and tentative voice, without quite realising what they were saying and doing to the mind of man, and often frightened of facing the consequences of their own theories. There were exceptions, men far-sighted enough to realise that the twilight of the gods was at hand, and foolish enough to shout it from the tree-tops—like that *enfant terrible*, Giordano Bruno, the Bertrand Russell of his age, who was burned alive. But when Copernicus

* William James, *The Varieties of Religious Experience*.

set the earth spinning, he did so with a timid and apologetic gesture; Kepler saved his faith by declaring that God was a mathematician by profession; Galileo's career was a life-long walk on a tight-rope; Newton wrote a treatise on the locations of Paradise and Hell; and at the end of the long chain Professor Toynbee claimed that the Catholic Church, possessing the ultimate truth, was quasi-exempt from the laws of history.*

Thus the new philosophy, with the exception of some of its more brutal propounders in the eighteenth and nineteenth centuries, made no frontal attack on religious beliefs; but it gradually undermined their foundations, on which all previous civilisations had been based. In the old days, man hoped to influence, through magic and prayer, the superior powers which decided his fate; now he could manipulate the mechanical components of his destiny, glands and humours, atoms and genes, and determine his own determinants. Prayer did not fall into disuse but its function, the influencing of fate, was taken over by the laboratories. Slowly but inevitably, divine providence was replaced by the drift of cosmic weather, ethical guidance by the ethical neutrality of science, humility before the supernatural by a feeling of arrogant, unlimited power.

Religion did not die, nor was it driven underground by the new philosophy—it was merely relegated to an airtight compartment of the mind, and sealed off from contact with logical reasoning. The incompatibility between the two halves of the split mind was smoothed over by the Churches' diplomatic appeasement of Science, and by the believers' psychological resistance against admitting the split. Yet in spite of these mental shock-absorbers, religion gradually lost its power, became brittle and fragmentary; once the controlling force of daily life, it became a spiritual luxury. The "oceanic feeling" could no longer

---

* *Civilization on Trial*, London, 1948, p. 238 ff. More recently, Professor Toynbee seems to have changed his view on this point.

fill man's horizon; it was preserved in a neat reservoir whose level kept steadily falling through drainage, leaks and evaporation.

Life was so exciting during these hectic, unprecedented centuries, that man did not realise what was happening to him. The navel cord through which he received his spiritual nourishment was shrivelling up, but there were plastic substitutes for it, and various forms of artificial nourishment. For a while the words *Liberté, Egalité, Fraternité*, produced a new magic, a seemingly apt substitute for the holy Trinity. There were breathtaking attempts to create a Humanist creed, and attempts to worship the Goddess of Reason; political movements and secular religions succeeded each other, exerting their immensely dynamic, but short-lived, appeal. The vertiginous rise of the power-curve was accompanied by mass-upheavals, ideological crusades and fanatical pursuits of Utopian mirages. Each of them promised a secular millennium, born out of a revolutionary apocalypse. Yet all the time, throughout these toxic excesses and spurious illuminations, there was a muffled feeling of uneasiness, of growing frustration, of spiritual desiccation. The explanations of science became more and more formal, non-committal and meaningless as answers to man's eternal question. As his science grew more abstract his art became more esoteric, and his pleasures more chemical. In the end he was left with nothing but "an abstract heaven over a naked rock".

8

With the beginning of the twentieth century, signs appeared which seemed to indicate an impeding turn of the tide. The descendants of Galileo and Newton found that they had been too optimistic in believing that the universe could be reduced to a mechanical model. The perfected measuring instruments signalled the presence of quantities and processes which not only eluded measurement, but by their very nature would always elude it. At nearly the same time, similar crises broke out in the other sciences: cosmology, biology, genetics, psychology. Physical determinism was shaken, rigid causality yielded to the elastic laws of probability; science had to admit that it can never predict, only guess, what will happen next. The living whole asserted its primacy over the measurable aspects of the parts; medicine had to lay increasing stress on the power of mind over matter. The most fashionable school of psychotherapy reverted to the Jamesian view that a transcendental faith was a biological necessity for man and that "the total absence of it leads to collapse"—the dark, feverish night of the soul.

Slowly, hesitatingly, the pendulum seemed to start swinging back; man seemed to be getting ready for a new shift of focus, a new mutation. But so far this has failed to materialise; and all attempts at a spiritual revival within the framework of the established Churches proved artificial and abortive. History may move in a spiral, but it never moves in circles, never returns to a previous point of departure. The physicist who has witnessed the collapse of his mechanical model of the universe has become a humbler and wiser man, but he cannot be expected to return to Aristotle's four elements and to Ptolemy's sky rotating on hollow crystal spheres; nor will the physician, who has learnt to accept his limitations as a healer, revert to a pre-Harveian view of the body. Yet the established Churches demand from all of us who shiver in the darkness, precisely that kind of intellectual suicide and surrender of the critical faculties. To ask twentieth-century man to believe in a loving God who condemns half his children to eternal damnation without hope of an amnesty, is really a bit thick. The reassuring statements of some modern theologians that Hell does exist but is empty, or that it merely means exclusion from grace without overheating, are hardly on a more adult level; and Mr. Greene's defence of the bodily ascent of the

The Failure of Response

Virgin in the pages of *Life* Magazine would embarrass even a saint. John Donne's "with a great, sober thirst my soule attends" was the statement of a perennial faith in the language of his time; "The Cocktail Party" in "The Living Room" is a parody of it.

Perhaps if Luther had been born after Newton, the gulf between faith and reason would be less disastrous. As it is, the established Churches are venerable anachronisms. They are capable of giving a limited number of individuals a limited reassurance and a limited, sporadic uplift; but the Sunday driver does not answer the need for public transportation, and a Sunday faith is no answer to the peril threatening our race. We may postpone the atomic Sodom for a few years, but we cannot indefinitely prevent it. Only a radical change of the spiritual climate could prevent it.

Unfortunately, changes of this kind, the next mutation, the next jump ahead, are not only unpredictable but beyond the power of imagination. The causes which lead to these extraordinary transformations of the global mood—the springtide of Christianity, the ground-swell of the Renaissance, the hurricane age of Science—are equally obscure, even in retrospect. Hegel's dialectic, Spengler's cycles, Toynbee's challenge-and-response patterns are beautiful prophecies in reverse—and as doubtful as all prophecies are, though they merely predict the past. The more we realise the infinite complexity of historic causation, the Nostradamus-in-reverse character of all philosophies of History, the more helpless we feel in trying to predict the next mutation. We can point to certain analogies, abstract certain patterns from the Persian carpet, isolate certain trends and chart their curves; the rest is guesswork, hope and prayer.

My own guess and hope, which I have indicated before, is the spontaneous emergence of a new type of faith which satisfies the "great sober thirst" of man's spirit without asking him to split his brain into halves, which restores the navel cord through which he receives the saps of cosmic awareness without reducing him to mental infancy; which relegates reason to its proper humble place yet without contradicting it. It all sounds very vague and irreverent, partly because we can imagine the machines, but not the beliefs of the future, and partly because we have become so accustomed to religion occupying one half of the split mind, that the idea of restoring its unity appears blasphemous. Is it really too much to ask and hope for a religion whose content is perennial but not archaic, which provides ethical guidance, teaches the lost art of contemplation, and restores contact with the supernatural without requiring reason to abdicate?

Clearly, the devout will regard this question as presumptuous and betraying a lack of comprehension for the revealed, or symbolic, or mystic essence of faith, according to his notion of it. "After all", he will say, with indignation, or contempt, or pity, "you cannot expect a religion made to measure like a suit, to satisfy your specific requirements." The answer, I submit in all humility, is that the indignation of one's Catholic, Protestant, Jewish and Moslem friends mutually cancel out; and secondly, that the objection is historically untrue. For every culture and every age did have its faith "cut to measure", and did re-state the perennial content of all religions on its own level, and in its own language and symbols. It is neither an irreverent nor an impossible hope that this will happen again in the future. But it *is* impossible to turn back to the language and symbols of a past epoch, of a mental climate which is no longer ours.

9

My starting-point was an imaginary chart, which showed a vertiginous rise of the power-curve coinciding with an equally unprecedented decline of the spiritual curve of living faith. It is this coincidence of the two curves which makes the present crisis so grave, which makes us feel that we are travelling at breakneck speed through the night with the throttle open at full and the steering broken down.

The decline of the spiritual curve remained for a long time hidden or obscured by more dramatic events; and its consequences have only become fully apparent in our day. When, a century and a half ago, the sailors at Spithead and the Nore started their famous mutiny, they took pains to assert their loyalty to the King, and to point out that they were merely rebelling against certain Admiralty rules. They continued to take the supreme authority for granted, and regarded themselves as His Majesty's loyal rebels. In a similar manner, the founders of new and reformers of old religions always took the existence of God for granted; they all were the Lord's loyal heretics. This seems to hold true for any period of human culture as far back as the beam of History is able to penetrate into the dark, and as far up towards the present as the beginning of the eighteenth century. At this point, the unique break occurs. God is dethroned; and although the incognisant masses are tardy in realising the event, they feel the icy draught caused by that vacancy. Man enters upon a spiritual ice age; the established Churches can no longer provide more than Eskimo huts where their shivering flock huddles together, while the camp fires of rival ideologies draw the masses in wild stampedes across the ice. Yet even this desolate state of affairs is preferable to the threat of the medicine men to remedy the climate by turning the frozen waste into a blazing furnace.

The horror of it is that they have the power to do it. If only half the official statements about the new nuclear and bacteriological weapons are true, then the next few decades, or the next half century at the utmost, will decide whether *homo sapiens* will go the way of the dinosaur, or mutate towards a stabler future.

We shall either destroy ourselves or take off to the stars. Perhaps the conquest of interplanetary space will cause a Copernican revolution in reverse, the emergence of a new type of cosmic consciousness. Perhaps the creation of artificial moons and similar toys will prove such an absorbing diversion that the old passions will be deflated, and their causes forgotten. Perhaps some unexpected discovery in the field of extra-sensory perception will provide us with a new spiritual insight, a new basis for our metaphysical beliefs, a new intuition of our ultimate responsibilities.

All this is vague and wild speculation, yet less wild and fantastic than what will happen to man if the near-miracle fails to materialise and the giant mushrooms start sprouting into his sky and lungs. The trouble with all near-miracles, such as our ancestors rising on their hind legs, or the rise of the new star over Bethlehem, or Galileo's climbing the towers of Pisa, is the unpredictability of their timing. Once we hoped for Utopia, now, in a chastened mood, we can at best hope for a reprieve; pray for time and play for time; for had the dinosaur learnt the art of prayer, the only sensible petition for him would have been to go down on his scaly knees and beg "Lord, give me another chance".